CREATIVE FAMILY HOME

Ashlyn Gibson

With photography by
Rachel Whiting

CREATIVE FAMILY HOME

Imaginative and original spaces for modern family living

RYLAND PETERS & SMALL
LONDON • NEW YORK

To Olive and my mum, for wrapping me
up in the wonder of creative family life.

Senior designer Toni Kay
Commissioning editor Annabel Morgan
Location research
  Ashlyn Gibson and Jess Walton
Head of production Patricia Harrington
Art director Leslie Harrington
Editorial director Julia Charles

10 9 8 7 6 5 4 3 2 1

Text © Ashlyn Gibson 2013
Design and photographs
© Ryland Peters & Small 2013

ISBN: 978-1-84975-439-2

First published in 2013 by
Ryland Peters & Small
20–21 Jockey's Fields
London WC1R 4BW
and
519 Broadway, 5th Floor
New York, NY 10012
www.rylandpeters.com

A CIP record for this book is
available from the British Library.

Library of Congress CIP data
has been applied for.

Printed and bound in China

CONTENTS   Introduction **6**

CREATIVE FAMILY STYLE **8**

CREATIVE FAMILY HOMES **42**

INTRODUCTION

I wanted *Creative Family Home* to be a style book that not only features outstanding interiors but also captures the innovative spirit and the nurturing soul of the modern family. It was important to select homes that are alive with inspirational ideas without being too aspirational or prescriptive – a creative family home isn't one that lifts its style from the pages of the latest interiors magazines. Rather, it is a work in progress, a place of originality and humour that is shaped by the children who live there as well as the grown-ups. A series of children's voices speak up throughout this book, telling us how they really feel about their homes and what is important to them.

In these pages, you will see iconic and contemporary design that comes with a price tag, but this is never the full story. These homes are beacons of originality, where ingenuity outshines big budgets and money plays second fiddle to imaginative flair. All of them incorporate clever ideas that can be adapted to suit your own home. You will find spaces where DIY style and flea-market finds sit alongside award-winning modern design, but running through each house is a vibrant sense of style, fun and warmth that is central to the creative family home.

My journey around Europe to the homes featured in this book has uncovered something new, visionary and exciting – a growing contemporary zeitgeist where children are encouraged to walk their own path, and where creativity and individuality reign.

CREATIVE FAMILY STYLE

CREATIVE FAMILY HOMES ARE AN ABUNDANT SOURCE OF PRACTICAL AND

INSPIRING IDEAS THAT CAN TURN DAILY LIFE INTO A COLLECTIVE ADVENTURE.

THEY OFFER ORIGINAL ANSWERS TO THE EVERYDAY QUESTIONS THAT ARISE

IN THE EVOLUTION OF ANY FAMILY ENVIRONMENT. PICK UP SOME TIPS ON

HOW TO REINVENT YOUR HOME AND ENJOY THE CREATIVE ENERGY AND

INDIVIDUALITY OF YOUR CHILDREN.

OPPOSITE ABOVE LEFT **I love to see new life being given to old-fashioned playground games. This indoor hopscotch makes an ingenious and irreverent use of a hallway and defines the family home as a place to enjoy.**

OPPOSITE ABOVE RIGHT **If you are lucky enough to have the space, a swing will change the tempo of your home and bring the spirit of outdoor play inside. As well as providing an exhilarating experience, it can also be a retreat for quiet contemplation.**

THIS PAGE **This is a democratic living space where every member of the family has an equal stake. A climbing rope introduces a challenging and playful dimension, while a playhouse is fun for the younger ones. This directional contemporary design also appeals to a grown-up aesthetic and blends perfectly with the family style.**

USING SPACE IMAGINATIVELY

WHEN WE WERE GROWING UP, MY
SISTER AND I INVENTED A STRING OF
SECRET CLUBS THAT WOULD MEET
IN DIFFERENT PLACES IN OUR HOME.
THE LABURNUM CLUB WAS UNDER THE
TREE IN THE FRONT GARDEN, WHILE
THE CUPBOARD CLUB WAS HIDDEN
AWAY ON THE LANDING. WE HAD SECRET
CODES AND SET OUT ON EXCITING
MISSIONS THAT USUALLY INVOLVED
SNEAKING THINGS OUT OF THE
KITCHEN AND BACK TO BASE.

Children love to make dens, to cosy up in small
spaces and to find secret bolt-holes they can call
their own. You don't need to invest in expensive
playhouses, which will soon be outgrown and have
a tendency to be over-prescriptive. Just provide
the basics, be inventive and take a DIY approach
to create interesting micro-environments that
will allow your children's imagination to flourish.

Space is often at a premium in a family home,
and if you don't have the luxury of a garden, you will
need to be imaginative. Bring simple elements of
the playground indoors to create a play place that's

RIGHT **A space that is too small for adults doesn't need
a "Keep Out" sign. A cosy burrow lined with a crochet
blanket and piles of cushions makes a quiet reading
corner to curl up in.**

fun and functional. If there is enough height, an indoor swing will give your children and their friends hours of enjoyment. A hallway can become a spooky tunnel or a passage into a magical land. The staircase can turn into an assault course or a mountain to climb. If you are short of space, improvize with everyday things or invest in a teepee that can be packed away at the end of the day.

Look for areas that aren't being used. We painted the walls of our porch with blackboard paint, to provide a space where the children are sheltered from the rain and can play outside close to home. With the aid of sheets and safety pins, the gap behind a sofa or the space under a desk can become a child's parallel universe, while a roll of masking tape can transform the hall floor into a hopscotch court for an impromptu game.

In the bedroom, invest in a raised bed, to provide more space for playtime, rather than a huge piece of furniture that dominates the room. When children outgrow the den they have created, it can be given a new purpose or reinvented time and time again. Wall space above desks and beds can act as a blank canvas and offers an opportunity to let your children create their own artworks.

All of these things will encourage your children to experiment and explore their worlds, and allow their imaginations to flourish.

ABOVE **Painting onto a wall may be anarchic, but it unleashes unprecedented self-expression. Working on a gigantic scale defined by masking tape allows children to lose themselves in the joy of creative exertion. Peeling the tape off at the end brings a magical moment of transformation infused with immense pride.**

LEFT **A blackboard is an inviting canvas for impromptu creativity. Nothing has to be permanent. It is a place to experiment where everyone can join in. Add a photographic element and you can build up a unique and fun family portrait.**

ABOVE Add your child's name to the wall by their bed to give them their own domain where they decide what goes! Allow them the freedom to experiment in their own space where they can begin to map out their world.

ABOVE RIGHT A hallway is transformed into a gallery of children's art. Give your children a week when they can display their own work and see how the energy of the space changes. Use Washi tape to make instant frames that are easy to remove.

RIGHT Move away from conventional blackboard walls and designate a piece of painted furniture as a blank canvas. The doors of a cupboard become ready-made frames for children to emblazon with their names and designs.

PRINT AND PATTERN

WHEN I WAS TEN, I EMBARKED ON A PROJECT WITH MY MUM. CUTTING PAGES FROM MAGAZINES INTO HEXAGONS, WE CREATED A KALEIDOSCOPIC PATCHWORK WALL ABOVE MY BED. I SPENT HOURS INVENTING STORIES AS I WANDERED FROM PICTURE TO PICTURE, LOOKING AT THE PATTERNS AND IMAGES. I'M NOT SURE THAT WE EVER FINISHED THE PROJECT, BUT IT WAS INDICATIVE OF MY MUM'S CREATIVE APPROACH, WHICH IS SOMETHING THAT STILL INFLUENCES ME TODAY.

The use of print and pattern will bring a light-hearted, colourful energy to a family home, capturing and inspiring your children's imaginations. Bold ideas, such as a dramatically patterned large-scale wallpaper, can inject a strong character into each room, or your home as a whole, but smaller touches, such as surface design on homewares and home furnishings, offer a simpler and less intimidating way of introducing idiosyncratic style to your space. Whether you choose an emblematic theme that runs throughout your home or take a more eclectic approach, print and pattern will add an individual touch.

Add screen-printed cushions, bold artworks and woven rugs to the living room; printed ceramics and melamine in the kitchen; colourful lampshades, bunting,

TOP RIGHT A bunch of printed paper lampshades creates a jolly mix of ditsy patterns. Each light hangs from a bright cord to generate the celebratory feel of party streamers. Frivolous and abundant, each one illuminates the space with a slightly different lustre.

CENTRE RIGHT A simple illustration is brought to life with colourful prints and fluorescent detail. A delicate decal of a bird perching on a branch decorated with Japanese kimono designs brings a touch of poetry to a plain wall.

BELOW RIGHT Create your own wall art by stretching printed fabrics over a box frame. The combination of pastel and primary colours in Karkuteillä, a stylized animal print from Marimekko, makes a dramatic contrast against the dark wall.

OPPOSITE A gorgeous mix of 1960s and 1970s wallpaper transforms an old wooden print box into a display case that has become an anthology of miniature worlds. Different motifs and designs in each compartment provide storybook backdrops for a collection of tiny toys.

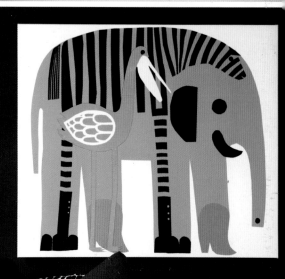

rugs and bed linen in your children's rooms; and patterned oilcloth on the kitchen table. And don't overlook the abundance of print and pattern in the everyday – graphics on packaging, stationery and stickers can all add layers of visual interest to your space.

Involve your children in the decoration of their own rooms and the rest of the family home. If you refuse to buy into mass-produced licensed products that enforce gender stereotypes – blue for boys and pink for girls – your children will be free to explore who they are and to find their own identity.

When it comes to choosing print and pattern, be inspired by your travels and the things you love, and treat your home as a project that will evolve as your children grow up. A colourful, visually stimulating home is full of possibilities and is an inspiring place for everyone, both adults and kids.

OPPOSITE ABOVE LEFT A clever 3-D quality has been given to a circus-influenced print by the repetition of the jovial spot motif in colour-coordinated lights. Monochrome harlequin cats introduce a different set of shapes as well as a comical surreal edge that appeals to adults and children alike.

OPPOSITE BELOW LEFT Fonts and illustrations on packaging are little works of art in themselves. Vintage tins and cartons are increasingly collectible and allow you to bring a bold graphic element into your home.

OPPOSITE ABOVE RIGHT Interesting patterns play games with the mind. This geometric wallpaper becomes a giant puzzle of shapes and colours that children spontaneously read in different ways.

OPPOSITE CENTRE RIGHT Develop an eye for customizing and embellish the mundane in your home. Vintage wallpaper creates a soft background for stylized face stickers that give personality to light switches.

OPPOSITE BELOW RIGHT One person's rubbish is another person's treasure! Don't overlook the everyday when it can be reused and reinvented. Decorate wooden vegetable crates with pretty patterns to transform them into colourful storage boxes.

ABOVE RIGHT A skull-and-crossbones motif is given a modern twist in an unorthodox colour palette. You can inject pattern into any space simply by adorning it with a string of bunting.

BELOW RIGHT Clashing patterns reflect how young children often dress themselves with a complete lack of inhibition. Follow their lead and customize wooden drawers with a brazenly eclectic mix of Pop-Art-inspired wallpapers.

STORAGE AND ORGANIZATION

STORAGE AND ORGANIZATION MAY SOUND DULL, BUT A HOME FREE OF CLUTTER WILL REWARD YOU WITH A CALM AND RELAXED VIBE. HAVING SPACE IN WHICH THEY CAN BE CREATIVE AND KNOWING EXACTLY WHERE TO FIND WHAT THEY NEED WILL ENCOURAGE SPONTANEITY IN YOUR CHILDREN.

Before you think about storing anything, consider whether you really want to keep it or whether it is, in fact, time to get rid of it. Having a good clear-out is a healthy and therapeutic thing to do with your kids. More often than not, it will induce interesting conversations about memories, or kick-start a game with something

OPPOSITE ABOVE LEFT Shop fittings make ideal storage solutions. A wire rack, customarily used for greetings cards, is a safe place to keep things with special significance.

OPPOSITE ABOVE CENTRE Exotic handcrafted woven baskets make lightweight storage for games, toys and books that can be picked up and moved from room to room.

OPPOSITE ABOVE RIGHT Transparent receptacles that are easy to access make storing possessions simple and straightforward. Storage systems with removable units are particularly handy if you need to transport the contents in order to work with them somewhere else.

OPPOSITE BELOW LEFT Pigeon holes decorated with black-and-white prints introduce a stylish design element to a simple and practical storage unit.

OPPOSITE BELOW RIGHT Old wooden crates arranged on a wall create generous deep shelving. When not used for storage, the crate on castors becomes a ride-on toy.

ABOVE RIGHT The Uten.Silo, an iconic moulded-plastic wall organizer, creates multiple storage options for all the family to enjoy.

RIGHT A reinvented vintage sewing box is the exactly perfect height and size for a child's book collection.

ABOVE **Finding coats and school bags in the morning can be the bane of family life. Give children their own peg and make everyone cultivate the habit of hanging things in their own place.**

ABOVE RIGHT **Translucent plastic crates in jolly colours reveal a helpful outline of their contents and help young children to keep things tidy.**

long forgotten. Don't rush your children – this is all part of the process of growing up. And when they are done, taking a big bag of things to a charity/thrift shop is good for the soul. Our clearing sprees often lead to a car boot/yard sale. Don't expect to make a fortune, but the kids will love it, and it will be a valuable exercise in freeing up space and letting go.

Once you have whittled down your belongings, think about the type of storage that your family needs. Make choosing what goes where collaborative and fun, rather than taking charge – this will encourage your children to take ownership of how their world is arranged. Everything should be easy to find and clearly defined. Children enjoy sorting things into groups or colours, so use that as a game when it's time to tidy up. That way, they will get into

the habit of enjoying the return to order as much as the happy chaos of playtime.

Look in junk shops and vintage stores for pigeonholes and furniture with lots of drawers that has been designed with organization and storage in mind. If you buy new and purpose-built storage, you can make it your own by customizing it. Portable storage, whether it is a box on castors or a vintage suitcase, is versatile and fun for children. For awkward nooks and corners, custom-built shelving and cupboards can offer perfect storage solutions and help to streamline your living space.

A well-thought-out storage system can be liberating and facilitate creativity. The imaginative energy of children will flow and resonate through the family home, filling it with life and vitality.

THIS PAGE **You can find the ultimate storage solutions in vintage outlets that specialize in old shop fittings. Designed with storage, display and practicality in mind, they can't fail to help with the organization of a family. Made with old-fashioned artisan skills and in quality materials, they become stunning pieces of furniture in their own right.**

OFICINAS

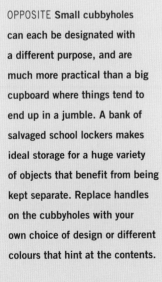

LEFT **Simple IKEA** cubbyholes provide the basic structure to develop a personalized storage system to suit almost any purpose. Indexed storage boxes, recycled wooden vegetable crates, wicker baskets and voluminous shopping bags all help to keep things in order.

THIS PICTURE **Be inventive with storage. A redundant supermarket shopping basket is an original and irreverent idea to introduce to the home. The handle allows children to easily transport objects from room to room and to sweep up art materials at the end of the day.**

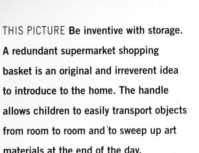

OPPOSITE **Small cubbyholes can each be designated with a different purpose, and are much more practical than a big cupboard where things tend to end up in a jumble. A bank of salvaged school lockers makes ideal storage for a huge variety of objects that benefit from being kept separate. Replace handles on the cubbyholes with your own choice of design or different colours that hint at the contents.**

ABOVE CENTRE RIGHT **Storage doesn't have to be dull. When edged with vintage lace, the shelves of an old cupboard give a fun and folksy feel to a basic children's wardrobe/closet.**

ABOVE FAR RIGHT **Don't throw away interesting tins and boxes that once contained craft projects or stationery sets. They can be re-employed to store personalized compilations of belongings.**

HOMEWORK AND CREATIVE ZONES

I CAN REMEMBER THE DESK I HAD AS A CHILD – A DARK WOODEN CUBE WITH THICK DOORS LINED WITH SHELVES. THERE WAS A PLACE FOR EVERYTHING, AND I LOVED IT. I SPENT HOURS SITTING AT MY DESK, WRITING IN MY SECRET DIARY, MAKING PLANS AND PLAYING GAMES. LEARNING SHOULD BE FUN, AND CHILDREN'S WORK IS TO PLAY AND TO IMAGINE. MY DESK WAS THE PERFECT PLACE FOR THAT!

There is something special about a child-sized desk teamed with the right-sized chair. With feet firmly on the ground, the child feels comfortable and in charge. Sitting and playing at their own desks encourages children to develop their powers of concentration, enabling them to zone out of the world around them and into their own activity. Becoming familiar with and enjoying their own organized space is also a good grounding for focusing on study when children are older.

ABOVE LEFT **A shelf fixed to the wall above a desk is an easily accessible repository for a personal library of sketchbooks and notepads. Such a well-organized and aesthetically pleasing place to work facilitates creativity and productivity.**

LEFT **An orderly desk is in striking contrast to the cloud of inspirational images and notes that billow on the wall above. The clean work surface encourages** focus and concentration, while the wall is like a thought bubble in constant flux.

OPPOSITE **The circus font on this poster declares the space a fun zone. An old school desk and chair have nostalgic charm, but blackboard paint turns them into objects that are always being redefined. A chalkboard on the inside of the desk lid is an invitation to make images as part of a secret world or private game.**

OPPOSITE **A mural of a cherry blossom tree under a full moon transforms an office into a magical place where ideas grow and imagination thrives. East meets West, and modern blends with vintage, to create a unique environment. A Roberts radio tuned into an Asian radio station adds another layer to the global mix.**

ABOVE **Get down to child's level with a single-storey cabinet for art materials. The surface is the perfect height to display the latest creations that children will enjoy looking at, too. The smears and smudges on paint pots and the splurging love of colour in children's art bring a vibrant note of liberation into family spaces.**

RIGHT **A set of iconic modular shelving from String comes with infinite possibilities. Suitable for any room, it can be added to, reinvented and transformed. Incorporating a modular desktop will transform a small area into a compact and organized study.**

There are many different types of desk available, for all kinds of spaces and budgets, ranging from the very simple tabletop on trestles to the more elaborate and mass-produced, as well as the custom-made or the vintage. Kids love nooks, crannies and cubbyholes, so choose a desk with drawers or use storage units (such as the little chests of drawers available at IKEA) to provide a handy space for everything. Create a brightly lit workspace by positioning the desk close to a window, or by adding a desk lamp or a strategically placed pendant light. Make the space inviting, with your child's name on the wall or the back of their chair. If possible, allow your children to use the walls around their desks like a noticeboard, where they can tape or pin up lists, pictures, postcards and other souvenirs.

A cupboard or a few drawers containing things you need for a creative session can be an integral part of any space, and once opened to reveal their contents, they will transform it into a little artist's studio. Putting out a small selection of materials will give an art activity focus and needn't take up lots of room. Allowing your children to be creative means accepting that there will be a certain amount of mess and that they will need to be encouraged to help tidy up. If you have access to an outside space, let your children use it freely for creative play. A simple box of chalks used on the pavement or an outside wall is a fun activity, and the artwork will wash away with the next rain shower.

ABOVE LEFT **A basic, child-sized desk provides a welcoming space with a sympathetic sense of proportion. The wall-mounted pots are big enough to hold generous handfuls of pens and pencils, making the impulse to draw irresistible, while a magnetic noticeboard lends itself to organizing ideas as well as creative play.**

LEFT **The improvised lettering makes for a wonderfully wholehearted announcement – this space has been named and owned, and everything made, written or drawn here will definitely be the product of a unique little creator! The heirloom desk carries the wear and tear of layers of creativity.**

It is easy to take a small-sized sketchbook and a mini set of pencils on any day out away from home. Don't buy a new sketchbook until the first one is full – this will encourage children to see a project through to the end and also to respect the value of their materials. When a sketchbook is finished, date it and put it on the bookshelf. Looking back at it when they are older will be enormous fun for you as well as for them, and will illustrate how bold and brilliant their art was before any inhibitions kicked in. If you don't have enough space to store or hang all of your children's paintings, take photographs of their favourites and submit them to a children's online art gallery, or save them in a dedicated file on your computer.

When my daughter Olive isn't playing at her own desk, she enjoys taking over mine. I love finding little notes that she has written in my notebooks when she has been playing, and it gives her a connection to my world, too. However, if you are going to desk-share with your kids, you need to be disciplined about putting your own important work away first. Being charged with respecting other people's possessions when in their space is a good lesson for children to learn.

If you let your children share your workspace, you will enhance the communal spirit of a happy family home. And if you give them a dedicated personal space of their own as well, it will help to develop their independence.

ABOVE RIGHT **Kitchen rails with pots and S-hooks are given a new context as storage for desk paraphernalia. They keep things within easy reach and help to keep the work surface clear. A pile of recycled boxes makes pretty and practical storage for all kinds of little projects.**

RIGHT **A reclaimed wooden desk, made by xo-in my room, has a solid and earthy quality to it. A mysterious world of figures and objects has been nestled against the back of the desk, but this still leaves plenty of space for working and creating. An orderly row of cubbyholes and drawers provides multiple compartments, putting fun into organization.**

CHILDREN'S CREATIVITY

GIVING A CHILD A WALL TO CALL THEIR OWN, WHERE THEY CAN EXPERIMENT WITH COLOURS, PATTERNS AND WORDS, WILL INSTIL A SENSE OF PRIDE AND PROMOTE SELF-BELIEF. SIMPLY LEAVE THEM TO IT AND WATCH THEM FLOURISH. A VIVID MEMORY OF MY CHILDHOOD IS A MURAL THAT MY SISTER AND I WERE ENCOURAGED TO PAINT ON OUR DINING-ROOM WALL. THE RESULT WAS SOMETHING UNIQUE AND IT BECAME A FOCAL POINT IN OUR HOME.

THIS PICTURE **Low-tack Washi tape is easy to peel off and comes in a multitude of colours and designs. Use it to stick pictures on walls without causing any damage or to personalize spaces and belongings by spelling out names or words.**

Games of make-believe, dressing up, story-writing, dancing, playing music and art all engage children in the act of expression and offer them something of great value that they can enjoy on their own without adult direction. While exploring their inner worlds, children learn the art of contemplation where they can unravel their busy little minds and learn about what surrounds them. Wrapped in their own imaginations, children can create a world that has great significance for them, that fills them with joy and that can be the pathway to their grown-up reality.

Don't be over-prescriptive but provide a safe environment for children to release their creativity. Teach them to embrace recycling and inventiveness by using discarded packaging as the basis for model-making. Art created from found objects can turn collecting into an artistic and creative activity. Invest in quality art materials if you can, have a special

OPPOSITE ABOVE LEFT
Give your children the materials they need to make an indoor rock garden. Planted with a few succulents it will make a fascinating landscape for a collection of toy dinosaurs.

OPPOSITE ABOVE CENTRE
Projects are a great way to engage children in creativity. Collect pebbles, then paint faces of smiley creatures and growling monsters on them.

OPPOSITE ABOVE RIGHT
Present your children's art on a rolling basis by investing in magnetic Perspex frames. They are quick to assemble and make changing the picture on display a weekly routine.

OPPOSITE BELOW RIGHT
Woodworking gives children the opportunity to make their own props. A set of tools and a measure of confidence will allow them to transform pieces of wood into swords or sculptures.

THIS PICTURE **Model-making is an activity that involves problem-solving and logical thinking. This wooden boat, crewed by a pair of penguins, also shows wit and ingenuity.**

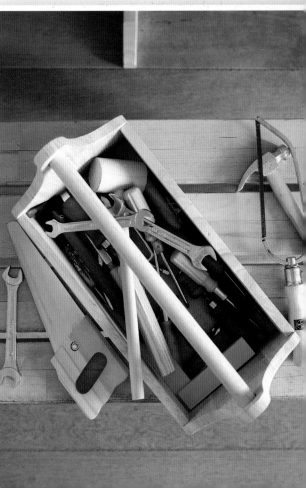

ASTRID LINDGREN   Han er her endnu - Emil fra Lønneberg   GYLDENDAL

JØRGEN CLEVIN   366 IDEER   BORGEN

DEN LILLE GRØNSPÆTTEBOG   VERDENS DYR   TEMPO

Rey • Rey   KRINGLE

UDE PÅ LANDET   CARLSEN

LEFT **Older children will enjoy learning the ancient and intricate Japanese art of origami. Multifaceted stars are just one of the many designs that can be made out of brightly coloured translucent paper. When placed on a sunny window, they play with the light like DIY stained glass.**

THIS PICTURE **Don't limit the colour of the paints to primary shades but invest in some rich and vibrant pigments that can then be used to create radiant works of art. Keep colours bright by providing each one with its own paintbrush.**

place to store them and encourage your children to clean brushes and put away paint and other materials carefully when they have finished. Try to resist the temptation to take over – encourage your children, but always allow them to take the lead.

Dressing up and playing make-believe is another aspect of creativity that will fire a child's imagination. Every home should have a dressing-up box containing a rich mix of interesting fabrics and discarded clothing and accessories. Capes, tutus, vintage headscarves, bags and hats all lend themselves to different characters. Don't fall into the trap of reinforcing little girls' yearnings to become pink princesses and boys to become superheroes. Instead, provide your children with a blank canvas that encourages them to create their own characters and to develop their own scripts.

OPPOSITE BELOW RIGHT **Handicrafts give children countless ways of making unique decorations for their rooms and an inexhaustible supply of lovingly made presents. A simple string of fairy lights customized with paper cups has become a joyful statement of individuality.**

ABOVE LEFT **Don't always hide art materials away or be too precious about the way they are stored.**

Simple glass jars with random handfuls of crayons and pencils, scissors and tape will give children different ideas about combining materials and media.

ABOVE **A wall covered with a family-sized pinboard becomes a project in which everyone can be involved. Children's art mixed with postcards and gift wrap creates a collage that expresses the style of the whole family.**

THIS PICTURE There is a simplicity and boldness to the impact of thick black line drawings. Invest in good-quality markers, but do insist that the lids always go back on! A row of medals repeats an interesting motif with random variations to create a really striking pattern.

Some creative activities are also a great way for children to let off steam when they are in a boisterous mood. Keep a basket of musical instruments to hand so that they can improvise with their friends and set off on impromptu parades. Part of the fun can be to make a selection of shakers from recycled materials and fill them with rice, bottle tops or tiny pebbles. Have fun, and remember – a creative world is a happy world to inhabit!

LEFT A collection of smooth flat stones becomes the pretext for a drawing game that experiments with human faces. Each stone becomes an individual character while different ways of simplifying facial features are explored. Naming each one and playing with them is an extension of the creative process.

OPPOSITE TOP RIGHT **A home-made stencil and a can of spray paint bring an anarchic element of street art into the home. A monster sticker adds to the identity that Oscar has created for the entrance to his own room.**

ABOVE **A toile tutu and a collection of necklaces are always at the ready for dressing-up games. Hanging from a length of string stretched across a wall, they add colour and excitement to the bedroom.**

RIGHT **Raw materials don't need to cost the earth. Take a thrifty approach! Reuse discarded packaging that your children can turn into models, and recycle paper that they can transform into works of art.**

THIS PICTURE **An assortment of trinkets and treasures sits together, as pretty as a picture, under a string of crochet bunting. A model of the Eiffel Tower is a happy reminder of a family holiday/vacation.**

THIS PICTURE **A collection of family heirlooms hangs on the wall to be enjoyed. Stories of three generations, each associated with a different handbag, inspire dressing-up games with a historical twist.**

COLLECTIONS AND DISPLAYS

AS A CHILD, I WOULD SPEND HOURS ABSORBED BY THE
CONTENTS OF MY GRANDMA'S BUTTON BOXES AND OLD
BISCUIT/COOKIE TINS. A MISCELLANY OF WATCHES, A
SOLITARY EARRING AND A BROKEN STRING OF BEADS
BECAME TREASURES IN MY GAMES OF MAKE-BELIEVE,
OR I LAID THEM OUT ON THE LAWN IN SUMMER, TO
CREATE MY VERY OWN CURIOSITY SHOP.

ABOVE RIGHT **A plywood display
box from IKEA provides a plain
and sturdy environment for a
parliament of owls. Symbolizing
virtues of wisdom and protection,
it is an endearing collection for
a family home.**

BELOW RIGHT **A set of pink
Russian dolls was the starting
point for Olive's collection themed
around colour. Whenever an "O"
is found, it is sprayed fluorescent
pink and added to the wall. A
line of clothes pegs sprayed with
the same paint and stuck to the
mantelpiece displays a range
of shiny treasures.**

LEFT **If you have beautiful things,
why hide them away? An Art Deco
shell light on a wall delicately
inscribed with the word "jewels"
becomes the site for a highly
original display of necklaces.**

Returning to my Grandma's treasures time and time again instilled rich memories that, even today, can evoke overwhelming feelings of nostalgia when I visit vintage fairs or look through her collections with my daughter Olive.

A collection can reflect a fascination with the ephemeral or the exotic, but it can also generate an appreciation of ordinary and everyday items. Collections convey personality and bring colour and narrative to a space.

Children are natural collectors, whether of sticks and stones from their immediate environment, or of something more eclectic, such as badges/buttons acquired during school trips and family holidays/vacations. Although a feeling of satisfaction may come from collecting sets of commercial memorabilia, such as sticker albums, this tends to make children consumers rather than creators. Their own magpie tendencies inevitably inspire more

ABOVE **A wooden pear criss-crossed with tiny compartments provides a curious means of display. A mysterious personal logic links the varied collection of nick-nacks and evokes an aura of romance.**

RIGHT **A collection of significant photographs casually arranged on a bedroom mantelpiece relates the story of a creative family. The multiple layers hint at its depth and richness.**

interesting collections, which place value on the ordinary and the everyday, and celebrate the innocence of childhood.

Children who collect things that really appeal to them frequently enter a wonderful world of make-believe. Far from simply acquiring these objects, avid little collectors also become absorbed in organizing and learning about their collections. They find connections and arrange the objects accordingly. Items in a collection can miraculously take on personalities and identities that stretch the imagination and lead to creative play.

Fused with enjoyment and excitement, the very idea of collecting is ongoing. To seek out additional pieces for a collection can become a lifelong pursuit. There is something magical about an inherited collection. As a work of art or a labour of love, it tells of someone's passion and can offer an insight into family history.

LEFT **A display focuses on family and folkloric tradition. A well-worn pair of child's lederhosen stands out from the wall like a museum exhibit. The heritage they evoke is picked up by little details in a collection of Polaroids framed alongside, which were all snapped on the couple's wedding day, when everyone dressed up in traditional costume.**

ABOVE **Cuckoo clocks make an entertaining display of a practical and educational nature. They provide a theme that could easily be pursued as an adult passion. Each one contains intricate traditional craftsmanship and unique variations that give them novelty status, making them fun and endearing to collect.**

Some collections stay stashed away like pirates' gold, ready for rediscovery and the invention of new games. Some breathe new life into vintage display cases, while others can provide a different purpose for a box or a container taken out of context and reinvented with an original twist.

Curating a collection is a wonderful thing that can inspire a deep interest in a subject or, perhaps, a simple fascination with the aesthetics of display.

RIGHT **A meticulously arranged geology collection, passed down through the generations, becomes a fascinating treasure chest. Each specimen has been identified, recorded and carefully exhibited in an old customized wooden cigar box. Inheriting a collection infused with passion is an object lesson in how to look after precious things.**

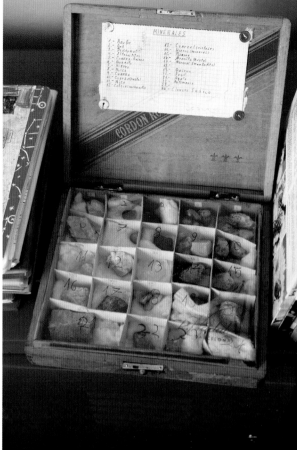

ABOVE LEFT **A prized collection of snow globes, displayed in the top of a vintage draper's cabinet, tells a story of many global adventures and creates a skyline of iconic sites from around the world. They are one of the cheapest souvenirs to collect yet one of the most inherently nostalgic.**

BELOW LEFT **A serried rank of Pez cartoon characters stands drolly on parade. Introduced in the 1920s, these plastic sweet dispensers, originating in Austria, have gained cult status among hobbyists. Far from being disposable or purely ornamental, they can be topped up with refills and reused.**

THIS PICTURE Children acquire lots of little things that can sadly become debris and easily forgotten. A miscellany of figures displayed in an old print box increases the enjoyment they give and encourages children to engage in playful activities with them.

CREATIVE FAMILY HOMES

IN ESSENCE, A CREATIVE FAMILY HOME IS EXPERIMENTAL AND ALL-INCLUSIVE.

YES, IT WILL BE STUNNINGLY DESIGNED, BUT IT WILL GO BEYOND SURFACE

BEAUTY TO EXPRESS SOMETHING AUTHENTIC AND UNIQUE ABOUT THE FAMILY

THAT LIVES THERE. ABOVE ALL, IT DEMONSTRATES THAT NURTURING A CHILD'S

WORLD IS AN ENRICHING EXPERIENCE THAT REAPS MANY REWARDS.

THIS PAGE **Olive's tricycle was a true investment purchase that has accompanied her way beyond its natural lifespan. Now almost too small for her to ride, it has become her circus horse as she balances on it and practises tricks. A favourite place to sit, she uses it as an extra chair with her legs dangling over the handlebars.**

OLIVE SAYS "I love collecting. I have my badge collection on the big lampshade. It's covered with souvenirs my dad brings back for me when he has been on tour."

ABOVE RIGHT **A patchwork of photographs creates a family montage stretching from floor to ceiling.**

BELOW RIGHT **The staircase is the natural place to leave your shoes at the end of the day. As you climb up, past brogues and brothel creepers, high tops and roller skates, you experience a very different kind of family portrait.**

VIBRANT VINTAGE

A BLACKBOARD-PAINTED PORCH, CHALKED WITH CHILDREN'S DRAWINGS AND NAMES, HINTS AT THE UNIQUE INTERIOR BEHIND THE SHABBY FRONT DOOR OF THE VICTORIAN TERRACED HOUSE IN EAST LONDON WHERE I LIVE WITH MY THEATRE-DIRECTOR PARTNER MATTHEW AND OLIVE, AGED TEN.

BELOW **A shopkeeper at heart, I have a penchant for old shop fittings, signs and displays. This draper's cabinet is a heaven-sent storage solution, housing all our art materials as well as piles of sheet music, stationery, stickers, board games and magic tricks.**

RIGHT **We live close to Columbia Road flower market and celebrate the changing seasons by filling the house with blooms snapped up just before the market closes. The mid-century desk in the hall can open out to create an extra workspace. A drawer from a junk shop is pushed underneath, creating extra storage.**

OLIVE SAYS "I love the gold frame in the sitting room. We decorate it in lots of different ways for parties."

My eclectic aesthetic and love of colour come in part from my own childhood in the late 1960s. Our home was punctuated with pops of colour, junk-shop furniture, bold prints evocative of the era and black-painted floors. Growing up in an environment where creativity was highly valued gave me a sense of freedom that is central to my own family home today.

Inspirational trips for my work take me around the world, and the new influences I encounter filter back into my everyday life. My ten-year-old daughter Olive loves to play with the collection of vintage

OLIVE SAYS "My friends love coming round to play. We have hula-hooping competitions and play games with Knightingale, my horse."

THIS PAGE Iconic Pistillino lamps from Studio Tetrarch transform this space in the evening, creating flower-like shadows in the alcoves of the dining room. The disused fireplace is home to a wood pile that feeds the open fire in the adjoining space.

THIS PAGE **A painting by Olive and a self-assembly cuckoo clock made from card hang next to a vintage clock found at a French flea market. The rubber kitchen floor from Dalsouple is in a shade of pink that I had custom-mixed to remind me of my travels in India.**

globes in our living room, which are a symbol of my wanderlust. A mission whenever I travel is to find one key purchase that will always evoke memories of a newly discovered place. A shell or a snow globe, an antique doll's head or a painting – it might be something simple or kitsch, odd or elaborate.

Far from traditional, the living space and dining room in our home are a riot of colour and pattern. The vintage carousel horse that occupies one corner was the starting point for a circus-themed space, reflecting a family passion for all things vaudeville and Olive's love of trapeze. Look in one direction and the bright living space is a picture of airy serenity.

LEFT **In the hall, a portrait wall runs from floor to ceiling and celebrates all that is good about family life. Favourite photos are printed on A4/US letter paper, then attached to the wall with spray adhesive – it's quick and it's easy. Friends love to check out the visual diary to see what's been going on recently in our lives.**

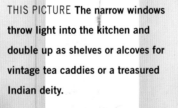

THIS PICTURE **The narrow windows throw light into the kitchen and double up as shelves or alcoves for vintage tea caddies or a treasured Indian deity.**

RIGHT **Our bedroom feels like a giant dressing-up box. A faded pink ballgown hangs in a gilt antique frame against a fluorescent pink backdrop, and old suitcases store festival clothes along with happy memories.**

BELOW **Poster-sized calendar pages run along the landing, mapping out dates to look forward to six months at a time.**

Turn the other way, and the vibrant geometric wallpaper throws a kaleidoscope of colour into the mix. A block of peacock blue fills an antique gilt frame and echoes the hue of the hall. Feeling nostalgic about my Indian heritage, I commissioned artist Bryony Lloyd to create a portrait of me for the living room wall that references my favourite country. Vintage tutus and sequined jackets hang on the back of the door, ready for a game of make-believe. The sofa, big enough to become a stage or an island, inspires hours of imaginary play. When it doesn't have a bunch of children playing on it, it's the perfect place to retreat to at the end of a busy day.

Around the dining table, old school chairs are painted in different colours, giving each one a playful character. For parties, we chalk names onto the backs of the chairs, which Olive and I customized with blackboard paint. I love the contrast of their utilitarian styling with the floral-printed 1960s swivel chairs at each end of the table.

Downstairs, the kitchen is home to all sorts of activities. Doors open out onto the garden, and Olive and her friends often dash in and out making secret potions in old glass jars. I love to bring the kitchen to life with vegetables piled up in fruit boxes and herbs bunched together like posies. The extendable round G Plan table

THIS PAGE **A drawer in a mismatched cabinet from House Doctor was repainted with a flash of fluorescent pink. Highlights of the same colour appear on printed cushions from La Cerise sur le Gâteau and hand-embroidered cushions from Rice. The panelled Victorian door, salvaged during a big renovation project, was left in its dilapidated state. In contrast, the Klimt-inspired wall decal inherited from a photo shoot adds a slightly surreal quality to the room.**

OLIVE SAYS "I like using my drums as little tables in my bedroom."

sits on a plastic woven rug from Rice to create a flexible and informal atmosphere, while Danish chairs covered in 1950s fabric throw another influence into the stylistic mix.

Olive's bedroom is a place where she can express her own ideas and aesthetic. She chose the colours for her room from my own Olive Loves Alfie eco-paint range and opted for Ghost Train, a warm shade of grey that's not traditionally associated with children's decor but is one that works really well here. Shocking pink Chinese lanterns and Russian dolls and a stark white oversized Miffy light stand out against the strong neutral background.

The use of rich colour and variegated pattern runs through our house, all the way to the main bedroom. Here, treasured heirlooms bearing the patina of time are combined with favourite pieces to create a haven of calm and curiosity.

In the summer, we like to open the French windows and spend as much time in the garden as we can. Outside space in a city is something that I really value, especially for children. Olive can plant bulbs and seeds, feed the birds and pick mint for her favourite herb tea. The high brick wall of the Victorian school next door gives privacy and a sense of magic to our outdoor living space. Vintage standard lamps light the garden at night, and an old leather sofa is our irreverent and very comfortable alternative to a traditional garden bench.

OPPOSITE **Children frequently accumulate too many possessions and their bedrooms end up choked with clutter. We try to have regular clear-outs so Olive has the space to enjoy the things she really wants to keep.**

BELOW **On a sunny day, the garden is as comfortable and welcoming as any room in the house. Pieces rescued from skips/dumpsters masquerade as garden furniture.**

ETERNAL SPRING

WHEN NADINE AND LARS WENT HOUSE-HUNTING IN EAST BERLIN, THEY DISCOVERED THEIR PERFECT HOME ON THE TOP FLOOR OF AN OLD HAT FACTORY. HERE, SURROUNDED BY THE SKY, EIGHT-YEAR-OLD LIO, NONO, AGED SIX, AND LILOU, AGED THREE, SIT HIGH ABOVE THE TREES IN THE SAFETY AND WARMTH OF THEIR FAMILY NEST.

To create extra space in their new home and to retain the feeling of light and height, Nadine and Lars built on an additional storey with floor-to-ceiling windows and a sunny roof terrace. Their bright, spacious apartment is full of reminders of the natural world, and there's always something seasonal on display, whether a simple bunch of spring flowers or a sculptural collection of twigs.

ABOVE LEFT **A Matisse drawing of a tree is the background for row upon row of photos that trace different branches of the family back to its roots.**

TOP **Wooden crates house an interesting shoe collection – clogs, ice-hockey boots and favourite sneakers.**

ABOVE **In this home, daily rituals are infused with fun and colour. Egg-cup characters display eggs marked with the children's names at breakfast time.**

LIO SAYS "I love my Mum and Dad's bedroom the best... no, the whole house. I love it all!"

CUISINE

THIS PAGE The open-plan kitchen is a nucleus around which creative activities ebb and flow. When the children take a break from the woodwork bench or drawing at their desks, they can clamber up onto the stools for a snack.

ESTCE
QUE TU
ME
T'AIME

OUTILS

NONO SAYS "I just like the feeling of touching the wood. Every time I finish something I have made with wood, I feel very happy with it."

howa

A powerful life force resonates through this home, and there is evidence of the children everywhere you turn. In the open-plan kitchen-dining area, polka-dotted letters spelling "cuisine" hang on the wall, adding a note of frivolity to the space. The centrally situated, island-based hob/stovetop turns baking and meal preparation into a sociable family activity. Everyone can take part, and it gives the children a healthy interest in food.

Alongside the kitchen area, both boys have their own desk, where they can create models and draw spaceships and time machines. Lilou also has a little table, which came from her grandfather's home. This has become her letter-writing desk, where she "writes" to her friends. Each child "owns" the walls around their desk, and they use brightly coloured Washi tape to stick up drawings, giving them a sense of pride in their achievements. Recycling items, such as egg boxes and paper packaging, are stored in a huge paper sack, just waiting to be transformed in the next art and crafting session.

OPPOSITE **The wooden workbench keeps the children occupied for hours on end. Instilling them with a sense of responsibility about how to use tools safely brings with it the freedom to experiment with child-sized saws, drills and hammers. A recycled glass jar full of plasters/Band-Aids is kept close at hand for any accidents.**

ABOVE **The boys each have their own desk by the window. An investment purchase for childhood, these desks have cleverly designed adaptable modular legs that can be lengthened as the child grows. Wide stools, big enough for two, encourage the boys to sit and make things together.**

LEFT **Old wooden fruit boxes and glass jars keep things organized. A hotchpotch of pens and pencils is at the ready for drawing sessions.**

NONO SAYS "I feel better when I look at the cherry tree."

LIO SAYS "It reminds me of spring."

At the other end of the kitchen, a wood workbench is the boys' pride and joy. Prolific and inventive, they make samurai swords and secret agents' guns for fantasy games. Their ingenious wooden models are scattered all around the home, on the mantelpiece and the walls, and as soon as the boys return from school, the home resounds with the noise of saws and hammers.

A celebratory atmosphere of springtime picnics reigns around the dining table, thanks to the large panel of cherry blossom wallpaper, vintage garden chairs and a long wooden bench. At the other end of this open-plan space is the cosy living area. Here, cushions and bolsters are

LEFT The wallpaper, with its life-size image of branches laden with blossom, was originally put up for a housewarming party but has become something of an emblematic image for the family. The image captures the spirit of *Hanami*, the tradition of picnicking beneath the cherry blossom trees in Japan.

ABOVE The family inherited a lovingly assembled collection of heart-shaped pebbles from Nadine's mum. Searching for new pebbles has become a regular family pastime that emphasizes the variety and beauty of nature.

covered with a variety of homey fabrics and are played with as much as they are rested on. The sofa takes on a new look almost daily as the children move the cushions around to suit whatever new game they have invented.

A staircase leads downstairs to the bedrooms and to a wide hall that has become a gallery of children's art. All three children share two rooms divided by sliding doors. Large fabric letters spell out

their names and demarcate their territory. Children respond with great excitement when the dynamic of a space changes, so when the dividing door slides back and the two rooms become one large playroom, there's a palpable sense of occasion. A child-height, lime-green border on the wall creates a magical zone underneath Nono's raised bed. The children love fantasy games and one of their favourites is to turn this space into the cockpit of their flying

ABOVE **When Lio was a baby, Nadine made him this model camera out of old cardboard boxes to explain that his daddy was a cameraman. Lio played with it for months and it has been repaired many times. The model has great significance for the family, as Nadine's father was also a cameraman.**

ABOVE **A memory wall is constantly updated with photographs that capture special moments. Tiny notes, drawings and pieces of paper with phrases coined by the children are also attached. The ever-changing display of family photographs is uplifting and life-enhancing for everyone.**

RIGHT **The oversized "pebble" cushions bring natural imagery as well as a sense of humour to the living space. Surprisingly soft and tactile, they tap into the children's imaginations with a longevity that extends far beyond most toys. When the children are tired, the pebbles are magical to fall asleep on.**

saucer. They use the white walls above their bed as a giant noticeboard to display whatever they like. Paintings are hung up to dry on a washing line around the top of the room.

Nadine and Lars' bedroom is the one room where the children didn't help to make decisions about the decor. Here, an atmosphere of simplicity and balance creates a relaxing haven for sleep and rejuvenation at the end of the day. The couple's love of nature is reflected in their choice of natural and organic materials.

This family home displays a wholehearted commitment to the creativity of children pursued through traditional play and crafting activities and low-tech natural resources. The result is a wonderful buzzy, inspiring home that changes every day.

NONO SAYS "The big pebble cushions are just cool, because they are great to play with."

NONO SAYS "It tickles me sometimes when I come home, because I am so happy."

RICHARD SCARRY
Le plus grand livre du monde

THIS PAGE **Sliding** doors transform the two children's bedrooms into a generous shared playroom. The space under Nono's bed is a favourite spot for imaginary games.

ABOVE The bathroom has been designed with children in mind. The child-height mirror is a clever idea that encourages the children to brush their teeth while having fun pulling faces at their own reflections. Old-fashioned drawstring bags printed with neon stars are used to store personal bits and pieces.

ABOVE RIGHT The main bedroom is a calm, almost monastic space. A natural linen bedcover, a simple wooden headboard and a collection of smooth stones give the space a Zen-like atmosphere of tranquillity. Tacked to the wall is a simple string of fairy lights in the shape of a heart, endorsing the family value of love.

RIGHT Lilou's Leander cot is as smooth and rounded as a well-worn pebble. Made from moulded beechwood, it is a work of art and a fine example of sustainable craftsmanship. Designed to adapt as children grow, eventually it will extend into a full-sized bed. It will provide a familiar environment right through childhood.

BAUHAUS BLESSINGS

KATJA AND FONS DE JONG TOOK RENOVATION TO EXTREME LENGTHS WHEN THEY BOUGHT A DECONSECRATED CHURCH WITH EVERYTHING STILL IN PLACE EXCEPT THE ORGAN. HERE, THEY HAVE CREATED A CALM, MINIMALIST HOME FOR THEIR THREE DAUGHTERS: 16-YEAR-OLD ZOE, 14-YEAR-OLD LEVI AND CECE, AGED 11.

Adhering to the Bauhaus philosophy that form follows function, everything in the de Jong home has a practical purpose. Whether vintage pieces or custom-built to fit the space, the furniture and fittings all celebrate craftsmanship. The minimalist approach means that the space is easily adapted for different seasons or occasions, such as birthday parties or family gatherings.

OPPOSITE **Cece loves to play with her Playmobil collection on the mezzanine above the kitchen. Her toys bring a strong element of primary colour and joy to the neutral palette of the home.**

BELOW **A mix of black-and-white photographs tells the story of different generations. The initials of the three girls have been chalked onto an unusual blackboard frame.**

BELOW LEFT **The church's antique pews have been recycled in many ingenious ways, including as shelving for the family's shoes.**

BELOW **Messages and affirmations are a fun and positive element to introduce into a home.**

Growing up in such an expansive space has been a treat for Zoe, Levi and Cece, who had the unusual privilege of learning to ride their bikes indoors, and the family still enjoys impromptu games of indoor hockey and football. Fons and Katja see the value of keeping their daughters' feet firmly on the ground and are great believers in counting their blessings. Old wooden letters spelling out "SMILE" are a reminder of how lucky they are.

In the main living space, a strong yet neutral colour palette draws inspiration from the original materials of the building. A narrow galley kitchen runs almost the entire length of the church and is divided by two tall, symmetrically positioned doors leading to the garden. The low ceiling created by a mezzanine level above the kitchen establishes a feeling of intimacy and gives it a very different ambience from the rest of the living space. Anglepoise lamps are

ABOVE **Industrial elements suit the scale of this space. Old factory lamps hang from the ceiling, while trolleys/carts on casters are piled high with magazines. The long, low woodpile creates a horizon, and the brick arch echoes the shape of the setting sun.**

FAR LEFT **Blue-and-white Japanese tableware introduces an exotic element at mealtimes.**

CECE SAYS "My older sisters love to play football. When I was younger I used to run around the house cheering in my sporting outfit, like I was going to play in a match with them!"

RIGHT **The girls each have their own deep drawers that they use as memory boxes. Easy access means they can dip in and out of photograph albums or look at their old school books whenever the mood takes them.**

BELOW **A wall-sized set of drawers works as a room divider and screens off an intimate lounge area within the vast living space. Stencilled numbers on the drawers introduce a graphic element that hints at its previous life as a stock cupboard.**

fitted to the walls at regular intervals to illuminate the kitchen shelves and steel worktops. It's rather like a laboratory where the children are encouraged to experiment with cooking.

At mealtimes, the family come together around a long table surrounded by a variety of chairs, including congregation chairs inherited from the church. Even though the girls all have desks in their own rooms, the table is also the favoured spot for homework, as well as a sociable place to gather at the end of the school day.

At the other end of the space, a raised area is home to a circle of comfy chairs strewn with cushions and crocheted throws, and arranged around an open fire. Design and travel books are stacked high as an alternative to a conventional library. There is a family ritual of gathering around the fire for the evening meal on Sunday evenings – a favourite occasion before the start of another busy week. Doors either side of the fireplace lead to the sleeping areas, and through the round porthole windows you can catch a glimpse of the bedrooms beyond.

CECE SAYS "I love it when my friends come for sleepovers. We play with my toys on the top bunks and have secret midnight feasts."

OPPOSITE **Cece's cosy whitewashed bedroom is flooded with sunlight. The lovely square space is dominated by the practical custom-built bunk beds that she used to share with her older sisters before they moved into their own rooms.**

ABOVE **Katja and Fons's bedroom feels rather like a log cabin, with a wood-burning stove and wood-lined walls made from recycled church pews. A false wall behind the bed conceals a small corridor that contains abundant storage.**

ABOVE RIGHT **A rustic table with a trio of lights creates a calm retreat in the master bedroom. The framed posters propped against the wall introduce an element of colour in a low-key way.**

At the top of a flight of stairs is the mezzanine level. This is entirely the children's domain and is filled with a random clutter of toys and games, including an old pinball machine. There are slouchy beanbags, a big, friendly sofa and a tatty old chaise longue where the girls can hang out, listen to music or watch movies with friends. Trestle tables are the base for an impressive Playmobil world that has evolved throughout three childhoods.

This family home could have been dwarfed by the grandiose proportions and broad expanses of the building, but Fons and Katja have succeeded in bringing a Zen-style calm to the space that chimes with the spirit of its original purpose. But there is nothing "holier than thou" about their willingness to allow their children to revel in the vast space and fill it with the joy of laughter

ABOVE **The family started to collect Playmobil when Zoe was younger, but Cece is the only one that still plays with it. She spends hours building fantasy cities and playing families, just like her two older sisters used to.**

LEFT The Polaroid family portrait wall is constantly added to, marking the changes in the children as they grow.

BELOW Flora and Alfred like to set the table for breakfast with their favourite Moomintroll mugs. Continuing the Scandinavian theme, the grown-ups have their morning coffee in Marimekko cups.

LEFT The Chief Steward's trunk is a family heirloom that has sailed the seven seas. After an eventful past, it has now found a resting place and is used to store a collection of accessories.

NORTHERN LIGHT

TO CREATE AN INSPIRING FAMILY HOME, SUSANNE BRANDT AND THOMAS RAVN MOVED FROM A LOFT IN A HIP URBAN NEIGHBOURHOOD OF COPENHAGEN TO A RENOVATED 1920S HOUSE. HERE, THEY HAVE CREATED A VIBRANT HOME FOR THEMSELVES AND THEIR CHILDREN, SIX-YEAR-OLD FLORA AND ALFRED, AGED TWO, WITHOUT COMPROMISING THEIR PASSION FOR CLASSIC DANISH DESIGN.

This bright and breezy family abode has a generous square layout that's typical of 1920s architecture. The open-plan ground floor conveys the feeling of a smoothly functioning home, achieved by removing all but one of the many original partition walls. An eco-friendly mix of modern and vintage lighting, controlled by high-tech movement sensors, illuminates Thomas and Susanne's assortment of much-loved mid-century Danish and contemporary furniture.

In the kitchen, predominantly black units provide a bold contrast to the whitewashed walls. There is a dedicated area for smoothie-making, a favourite family activity that starts the day in a healthy way.

THIS PAGE **At mealtimes, the family gathers around the Corona table by Dom Italia. The single moulded leg is stylish and practical, as it allows extra space for visiting friends and family. The iconic Panton chairs sit neatly next to the Stokke Tripp Trapp highchairs, providing classic seating for both generations. The Moon-Lamp, an early Verner Panton luminaire, bathes the table in adjustable and atmospheric light.**

FLORA SAYS "I love our living room because that is where we all play different things together."

THIS PAGE **A light and airy space dedicated to children's play is integral to the living area. A Schylling Speedster Race Car is at the ready for an impromptu car chase. On sunny days, the doors can be thrown open and the children's table and chairs moved outside, making the deck into an extension of the play area.**

THIS PAGE **Throughout Susanne's home, cheerful colours and contrasting textures pop against clean white walls. The Stingray rocking chair by Thomas Pedersen is a favourite with the children, and a pair of leather Corium lights designed by Pernille Vea adds warmth to this corner.**

All the children's tableware is stacked on child-height shelving, which encourages Flora and Alfred to contribute to family life by helping to set the table. Injecting an element of fun and ritual into daily chores gives the children a sense of routine and responsibility that they can enjoy.

Custom-built units line the walls in the living area, creating a broad shelf that runs around the room and is within easy reach of little hands. Here, favourite toys sit alongside framed pictures and letters salvaged from vintage shop signs. The cupboards below provide storage as well as exciting hiding places for the children.

THIS PAGE **The big picture window creates a light-filled screen between the main living space and the lobby. A trio of timeless glass pendant Mega Bulb lights by Sofie Refer gives focus to a corner of the living room.**

The white walls and painted wooden floors of this home epitomize the Scandinavian look and create the perfect backdrop for Susanne and Thomas's collection of contemporary art. The children's pictures have also been framed and hung alongside works by both up-and-coming and more established artists. Around the corner from the dining area, the capacious sofa is a focal point for the family at the end of the day, and the wood-burning stove gives the living space a heart-warming glow.

Susanne encourages Flora and Alfred to be creative by making sure they are not over-stimulated. By focusing on a different activity every few weeks, the children thrive in a harmonious space that isn't cluttered or over-populated with toys and games. The play area might change from a miniature library to an artist's studio or the setting for a magical tea party, initiating creative play for all the family. French windows either side of the play area lead to a small city garden where the children engage with nature.

ABOVE **The family art and memorabilia displayed in the hall make it feel more like a room and less of a transitional space. Susanne and Flora hunt out vintage toy cars for Alfred on their visits to flea markets.**

BELOW **Supporting contemporary designers and buying sustainable products are high on Susanne's list of priorities. Lilly's Chair and Geo's Table by Danish company We Do Wood are investment pieces that will stand the test of time. When Alfred gets too big to use the table as a desk, it can be used as a side table.**

ABOVE **In the master bedroom, print and pattern evoke a playful, child-friendly vibe that appeals to the whole family. Susanne bought the quirky knitted sculpture of giant beads from a Danish design store after it had been used in a window display. Suspended from the ceiling, it adds a note of humour to the bedroom. Full-length doors open onto a balcony with potted olive trees. This is a popular spot to hang out when the sun is shining.**

Recognizing that children have hectic lives too, Susanne has made sure that Alfred and Flora's bedrooms are cosy and peaceful as well as providing an inspiring environment for play and creativity. She has used different light sources in their rooms to create zones for reading, writing and playing.

Whimsical prints and painted floorboards give each of the children's rooms their own character. By making use of under-bed storage, games and toys are rotated to keep them interesting. The landing has been given a playful twist with a vinyl hopscotch court that the children and their friends love to use.

Susanne tries to avoid mass-consumer culture by taking Flora to local flea markets to get her fix of plastic kitsch. Following a philosophy of "one in, one out", each new treasure replaces something that is sold or passed on to a lucky recipient.

In the main bedroom, a charming collection of home-made family treasures in a simple Perspex box takes pride of place on the wall above the double bed. In many homes, these treasures would fail to find their way into a "grown-up" space. The cheerful sunshine-yellow floor gives the room a feeling of vibrancy and joy that the children love.

A vintage shelf unit is perfect for displaying a selection of Alfred's books. A collection of cushions gives the bed a cosy feel, while the trio of Flower Pot lights by Verner Panton provides just the right ambience for a favourite place to sit and read. The old-fashioned hobby horse underlines Susanne's preference for traditional toys that leave more scope for imaginative play.

ALFRED SAYS "My bedroom is full of my favourite things and my favourite colours, so I love to play there."

THIS PAGE **The Arco light is known as the "disco light".
The boys love to crank up the music after supper and
have an energetic half hour dancing around the table,
each enjoying their moment of fame in the spotlight.**

ART HOUSE

THE LONDON HOME OF GARTH AND LOUISE JENNINGS RESONATES WITH THE SOUND OF PLAY AND LAUGHTER FROM FOUR LIVELY BOYS UNDER THE AGE OF TEN: OSCAR, LEO, CASPAR AND ASA. THE FAMILY WALKS ITS OWN PATH AND ENCOURAGES SELF-EXPRESSION.

LEFT **A blackboard chalked with a heart design provides a dramatic backdrop for this portrait wall of family photographs, mostly taken in photo booths. The wall has become an ever-changing work of art.**

BELOW FAR LEFT **An old shoeshine box is the perfect place to store a selection of family shoes. With her eye for a bargain, Louise picked up the box for a song from an antiques fair at the end of the day.**

BELOW LEFT **The wall in the hall is punctuated with coat hooks that resemble giant yellow Smarties/ M&M's. Fun but practical, they provide just enough room for the coats and hats of the moment.**

OSCAR SAYS "I like this house because it was built in the Victorian times. That means I can spend a lot of time ghost-hunting!"

OPPOSITE **Humour anchors a daring mix of styles in the living space. The oversized modern floor light from Moooi is a fun and witty play on proportion. A collection of faux blooms arranged in blowsy bouquets evokes a tongue-in-cheek sense of grandeur.**

RIGHT **The rooms on the ground floor are all given different moods by introducing a variety of textured flooring in different colours. Patricia Urquiola's quirky Mangas Globo rug brings humour and an artisan feel to the music room.**

BELOW AND INSET **In most homes, drawing on the wall is considered a crime, but here it is a means of expression to be celebrated. Louise's felt-pen drawing entitled "My Family" was the gesture of a moment, but it captures the creative spirit at the heart of this family.**

Behind the offbeat green front door of the tall Victorian house, the Jennings' home is in a glorious state of evolution. It is also a glowing example of a family home that captures a spirit of wonder and discovery. Music, storytelling, drawing and design make up Garth and Louise's work, and it's immediately evident how their creative interests influence the choice of play of their four young boys.

Each and every wall in the house displays an eclectic collection of much-loved pieces that draws you into the Jennings' world. Favourite books and other treasures nestle alongside vintage finds and family photos, each item telling a story and creating a unique family style. Purposeful but not precious, there is a strand of humour that runs through this home from top to bottom.

Framed by a wall of bookshelves, the living room is a relaxed and cosy space in which to curl up and read a book or hang out with the rest of the family and watch a movie. A cornucopia of styles – 1930s armchairs, a collection of graphic contemporary cushions, an elegant vintage chandelier and a huge convex mirror over the mantelpiece – sit happily together, despite

ASA SAYS "It's a magical room that is small and cosy. I like hiding away in it. It feels like a forest den."

referencing several different eras. The adjoining living room is home to Garth's piano, ukulele and guitar, and is often used as a music room. Music is a major part of this family's life, but this is less a space for formal tuition and more one for spontaneous music-making.

Large skylights and an extension at the side of the house have opened up the ground-floor space. Retaining the original full-height shutters at the back of the living room provides a grandiose sense of proportion before you step down into the retro-inspired kitchen-dining room. To add an element of fun, Louise has sourced an eclectic mix of chairs that creates an interesting patchwork of colour and style around the table. Each member of the family naturally gravitates to a different style of chair. For this space, Louise chose a child-friendly Dalsouple rubber flooring that is hard-wearing enough to withstand bike races around the kitchen table.

Upstairs, the master bedroom doubles as Garth's workspace. An old school desk sits in one corner, and a selection of pictures hangs in a constantly evolving display. In the same manner, frames and other objects are propped up on the mantelpiece, evoking memories both recent and distant.

The children's rooms are all very different but add further charm and interest. Thanks to a bold choice of wallpaper, Asa's room is wrapped in an enchanted black-and-white forest landscape where it's easy to imagine disappearing for hours into a world of make-believe. Louise has a collection of sewing boxes, picked up from car boot/yard sales, that she uses as side tables and toy boxes throughout the home, and Asa's book box is a perfect example of her imaginative approach to storage – taking items out of context and reinventing them is a key part of the irreverent aesthetic of this family home.

OPPOSITE **The Woods wallpaper by Cole & Son in Asa's room creates the feeling of a mysterious domain where storytelling is king. Accents of fluorescent colour and clashing pattern lift the space and introduce an element of fun and frivolity. The framed Moomin illustrations by Tove Jansson pay homage to classic children's stories.**

A cosy sofa, just big enough for two, creates the perfect place for storytime at the end of a busy day.

BELOW **Camouflage letters spell out Asa's name and proclaim him ruler of his imaginary kingdom. A child-sized bookcase in the shape of a birdhouse provides a home for special things.**

LEFT AND ABOVE **Louise and Garth's bedroom has a hint of 1930s elegance, thanks to the delicate anemone motif wallpaper from Neisha Crosland. The disused fireplace is a good home for books. The blue eiderdown was bought from a market stall on a freezing cold day when blankets seemed like the thing to buy! It is used by everyone in the family when they're feeling a bit low and want to wrap themselves up in something that feels like home.**

Vibrant yet serene blue paint, mismatched salvaged letters spelling out his name and an old wooden crate turned into a shelving unit give Oscar's room interest and personality. Pursuing a love of music, he loves to escape to his own space to practise the trumpet. In Leo and Caspar's shared bedroom, their bunk beds provide a stage for all sorts of imaginary games, while the ghostly Cow Parsley wallpaper from Cole & Son gives the space an unexpected twist. It was chosen in the hope that it would inspire the boys throughout their childhood and grow with them, rather than being quickly outgrown as so many children's wallpapers are.

RIGHT AND OPPOSITE **Caspar and Leo's bunk beds are a starting point for imaginative adventures that spawn makeshift dens. By the end of the day, these are ready to collapse, clearing the space for tomorrow's games. The use of clashing prints gives the room an irreverent feel and a wacky sense of humour.**

CASPAR AND LEO SAY "Our room is the monster office. You're only allowed in it if you know how to make dens and create monsters!"

OPPOSITE **A crocheted blanket provides a traditional aura of comfort in Oscar's room, together with the vintage school desk and chair, which were car-boot/yard-sale treasures – Oscar loves the fact that they both have private storage compartments. The exposed pendant light, with its slight Heath Robinson feel, gives the room a modern spin, as does the simple IKEA storage unit personalized with a découpage of comic-book tearsheets.**

THIS PAGE **The family bathroom has a sense of grandeur, with a huge free-standing claw-foot bathtub that's the perfect size for a family with four children. Having taps/faucets in the middle means there are no arguments about who sits at which end.**

THIS PAGE The crimson kitchen wall, framed by a wide opening from the dining room, introduces a plane of bold, vigorous colour. An old kitchen cupboard, full of china and tableware, stands conveniently to one side. The two woven storage baskets on top make the most of the available space.

BELOW **Retro-inspired Formica Bambi coat hooks from Pakhuis Oost bring a whimsical air to the hall. By keeping hats, coats and bags off the floor, the hooks also create a sense of space and stop things from getting lost.**

LEFT **A framed montage of Polaroid photographs from Nici and Knut's wedding hangs in the dining room. It is an emphatic celebration of family and friendship, and a joyful reminder of Nici's Austrian heritage.**

BELOW **Nici collects enamel plates, which remind her of her grandmother's home. A variety of new and old pieces creates a wonderful mix of patterns. Colourful and unbreakable, they are the perfect choice for family tableware.**

HEARTFELT FOLK

NICI ZINELL AND HER HUSBAND KNUT HAKE ARE PASSIONATE ABOUT CREATING A WARM AND WELCOMING HOME FOR THEIR THREE CHILDREN: ZIZOU, AGED EIGHT, ZÖE, AGED FIVE, AND TWO-YEAR-OLD ZAVI. THEIR SPACIOUS APARTMENT IN BERLIN IS SURROUNDED BY PLAYGROUNDS AND PARKS, WHICH PROVIDE THE OUTDOOR SPACE THAT CHILDREN NEED IN ORDER TO FEEL FREE WHILE LIVING IN A BIG CITY.

From the square-shaped hallway, large double doors lead to an expansive dining room. This is the heart of the home and also the largest room in the house, where visits from friends, children's parties and lively indoor games all take place. The children have plenty of space to ride their bicycles or chase each other around the dining room table, with the sturdy hardwood floors able to withstand the rough treatment. Quieter pursuits are also undertaken here, whether working on school projects or doing enormous jigsaw puzzles.

There are shades of a traditional drawing room in the arrangement of two sofas in the dining room, but this space is also full of life and adventure. The children like to build dens

ABOVE **Nici has been collecting hand-carved wooden animals for over 20 years. Made from organic wood and painted with vegetable dyes, the animals are safe for the youngest of children to play with. Their simple shapes leave room for little imaginations to flourish.**

behind the furniture or lose themselves in storybooks, curled up among the cushions. One of the sofas was re-covered in a rich crimson fabric that became the inspiration for the large blocks of flat colour that run throughout the home. Shades of red, from cadmium to vermilion, work with the dark wooden floors to draw the space together and give it both harmony and vitality. Hints of Nici's Austrian heritage pop up throughout, and hanging on the dining-room wall alongside wedding photographs is a pair of vintage children's lederhosen.

The dining room leads to a cosy corner room that is flooded with natural light. Here, two ebony-black walls absorb the daylight,

creating an intimate space that is home to the voluminous family couch. On lazy afternoons, there is enough room for the whole family to fall asleep in front of the wood-burning stove, read or play games.

Nici grew up experiencing many different styles and cultures and has used items from all over the world to perform functional tasks around the home, making them intrinsic to the family style. In the tomato-red kitchen, for example, a cosmopolitan collection of tins is a fun way to store mundane items from dishwasher tablets to teabags, and puts a creative twist on utilitarian needs.

The corridor to the bedrooms has two-tone walls with dark grey on the lower section and

THIS PAGE **In the dining room, a single red Tripp Trapp chair, a Russian doll on top of the wall cabinet and a melamine cup on the table all echo the recurring colour theme of the house. The big family fridge is decorated with drawings and a series of hand-printed luggage labels. Left over from home-made Christmas wrapping, these spell out the children's names.**

LEFT **A Scandinavian wood burner throws out an intense glow that contrasts beautifully with the dark walls in the family room. Against this backdrop, a Marimekko canvas brings vibrancy and a colourful touch of childlike humour to the space.**

RIGHT **A wooden car, originally bought as a Christening present for Nici's oldest son 20 years ago, is still going strong. This beloved veteran has clocked up literally hundreds of miles and become a treasured possession.**

white above. The colour blocking is continued in the children's bedrooms, where grey is replaced with blue, pink and a paler grey on the lower part of the walls. It's a simple and effective idea that gives the rooms an increased sensation of height and a distinct "line" along which the children display favourite things.

Zizou's room is a magnet for his younger siblings, who love playing there with him. Their big brother is very much the explorer, organizing imaginary voyages where his bed becomes a pirate ship and the top of the blue wall is the distant horizon. A collection of trophies from their adventures decorates the wall: a pirate flag, photo-booth snapshots, a candy bag with a secret stash and twigs wound up in string and postcards.

Zöe and Zavi share a room that is divided by the clever use of colour. The very different feel that exists on each side of the space creates two distinct zones, which the children have stamped with their own personalities. Zöe's corner is adorned with pops of fluorescent colour in the form of an ABC poster from Dandy Star,

ABOVE **The children's twig collection has been turned into a Shinto-style shrine to nature, adorned with photographs, dainty miniature pompoms and Chinese lanterns.**

ABOVE **Different-coloured baskets help the children to remember what is stored where. Tucked neatly under Zavi's bed, they are easy to pull out at playtime. A brightly printed play mat doubles up as a fun and vibrant rug.**

BELOW **The bathroom is representative of all the family. Nici's jewellery collection hangs on the wall, bringing colour and a dash of glamour to the space. At the far end, an old-fashioned wooden boat and a miniature watering can are ready for bathtime games.**

a strip of bunting and brightly printed bedding. Classic modular shelving from String, which can be adapted and extended in all directions, lines half the room. Crates, boxes, mini-suitcases and baskets are lined up on the shelves, filled with art materials, musical instruments and dressing-up clothes.

Taking its cue from the vibrant glow of the wood-burning stove, this home revels in sensual textures and vibrant colour combinations, as if to wrap all its inhabitants in warmth and joy. Nici's eye for detail, her knack for creating physical comfort and the whole family's readiness to have fun make this home a deeply nurturing environment.

ABOVE **The old sports locker, battered with wear and tear from a previous life, was inherited from Zizou's dad and gives his room a boyish feel. Aluminium trunks from Zarges, which are used by film crews around the world, make perfect and playful storage boxes for children. They are light enough to be moved around yet strong enough to stand on.**

ZÖE SAYS "I have a suitcase full of dressing-up things and I like to dress up as a princess but also a pirate."

THIS PAGE A mix of new and old comes together in Zöe's corner of the room to evoke a sense of nostalgia with a modern twist. A fold-away mattress slips under the bed, at the ready for sleepovers or games of roly-poly.

A B C D
E F G H
I J K L
M N O P
Q R S T
U V W X
Y Z

CATALAN CURIOSITIES

IN A QUIET NEIGHBOURHOOD OF BARCELONA, RICH IN ART NOUVEAU ARCHITECTURE, CARINA HEMMINGS AND JUAN CARLOS PONSA HAVE CREATED A UNIQUE HOME WITH THEIR FIVE CHILDREN AGED BETWEEN SEVENTEEN AND TWO: OLIVIA, IRENE, VICTOR, PABLO AND THEO.

THIS PAGE **Traditional Spanish design is rich in pattern, and this is reflected throughout the house. It's an ideal vehicle for the introduction of a subtle range of colours and intricate motifs.**

Carina and Juan Carlos have a curatorial flair. They don't decorate so much as arrange, creating displays and assemblages throughout their home. Collections of paintings, coral, fish motifs and colourful glass generate an exuberant sense of style. Stories about the curiosities they have bought feed the children's imagination and foster a fascination with history.

The entrance to the apartment leads into a small lobby area. Deep olive-green walls are warm and welcoming and create an atmosphere of anticipation. A large mirror, picked up at a flea market, is used as a noticeboard for photographs, tickets and flyers.

THIS PAGE Lighting from different eras brings character and warmth to the living room and makes it easy to create various moods. The robust wooden star lamp, with a suggestion of Hollywood glamour, is in strong contrast to the delicate antique chandelier and the minimalist standing light by Franco Albini.

OPPOSITE AND ABOVE **In the kitchen, a collection of mismatching and random vintage glasses is displayed on glass shelves. Children's drawings and paintings are simply stuck to the cabinet doors – a simple and easy way to inject colour into the home and to instil children with a feeling of pride in their creations.**

The marble top of the console table beneath was cut to fit a set of ornate table legs discovered in an antiques shop, creating a unique piece of furniture.

The apartment was originally composed of many small rooms, each with a different tiled floor. Carina and Juan Carlos completely reinvented the space by knocking down dividing walls to create large, light-filled rooms. Accordingly, the flooring in the apartment is an eclectic patchwork of differently patterned tiles.

At one end of the long hall, sunlight shines into the open-plan living space. An oversized antique map of Italy is the dominant feature here. Juan Carlos used to tell the children that his ancestors were pirates from the Italian island of Ponza, so he bought the map to show them where it was. When he and Carina were renovating the apartment, they uncovered the bare plaster wall behind a partition. Now its patina of age gives the space soul.

In the dining area, the dining chairs are a mixture of different styles, reflecting the varied display of paintings and objects around the fireplace. Material rescued from an antique fabric shop that was closing down has been used to upholster a curvy 1950s chair and cover a made-to-measure pendant light hanging above the table. A typically Spanish 1970s bedspread has been used as a charming and eccentric tablecloth.

When their youngest child, Theo, was born, Carina and Juan Carlos created space for a new kitchen by glassing in their balcony. Losing the outside space to gain an extra room was a relatively easy decision

ABOVE **In the entrance hall hangs a string of faded bunting made from a collection of vintage travel pennants promoting the beauties of Cannes, the Côte d'Azur, Paris and Rome. When on their travels, it's become a tradition for the family to look out for more pennants to add to the bunting when they get home.**

ABOVE **Carina likes to make her own partyware and for each celebration she and the children come up with new designs. For Theo's second birthday, they made conical paper hats in sherbet colours trimmed with pompoms.**

OPPOSITE **A model of Doraemon, the time-travelling Japanese anime character, sits on the dining room mantelpiece alongside treasured artworks by the children. The other pieces on display are by unknown artists and all inexpensive. Creativity in all its guises has intrinsic value to these avid collectors.**

to make. When the sun is shining, the family head straight for the beach, and on duller days they still have an incomparably bright and airy kitchen. On the walls, glass shelves salvaged from an old-fashioned sweet shop/candy store have been given a new incarnation. A single jar of sweets/candy is a symbolic reminder of the shelves' origin, while a collection of Japanese fish vases symbolizes good fortune. Paintings don't need hanging space in this home – they look just as good when propped up on shelves and worktops.

A long corridor leads to the bedrooms, each of which has a very different ambience. The bleached colours of an old Ektachrome print create a dreamy atmosphere in 14-year-old Irene's pretty, feminine bedroom, where a study area

PABLO SAYS "It makes me feel important when my mother puts a drawing I made at school next to the paintings, photos and sculptures above the fireplace!"

THIS PAGE **A bunch of Japanese paper lampshades tied together with ribbons illuminates Irene's room with a delicate glow. The bed was designed especially for the space and incorporates lots of storage. A small den underneath, made homey with crocheted blankets, piles of cushions and a toadstool lamp, is a favourite hideaway for Irene and her little brother Theo.**

IRENE SAYS "I love my bedroom because it's original and different from the others. It's the place where I can have my stuff and be alone for a while."

with a wooden desk made from reclaimed wood and full of compartments provides a perfect place for reading and homework.

Further down the narrow hall, the space broadens out into the master bedroom. Here, old wooden doors brought from Juan Carlos's family home have been used as a headboard, providing warmth and depth, and introducing a rustic note to the space. The geometric design of the Union Jack cushions, emblematic of Carina's British heritage, add a touch of colour and contrast. Stacks of books and magazines are piled up on stools and old wooden chairs, within easy reach of the bed.

The adjoining room, reached though sliding doors, is little Theo's bedroom. Original drawings for wallpaper designs hang in box frames that are wide enough to have toy animals perched on top. Family photographs, drawings and a string of coloured lights are stuck to the wall in haphazard fashion, giving the space a lively energy.

This is an intriguing family home, full of life and soul, where there is enough room for everyone and everything. Being surrounded by so many interesting objects, each with its own history, provides constant visual stimulation for the five children, who are growing up absorbing a love of original art and design because it's right at the heart of their family home.

LEFT **The traditional tiled floor in the master bedroom is typical of the Art Nouveau architecture that characterizes this area of Barcelona. It creates a border of muted blues and earthy tones around the bed, like an elaborate Persian carpet.**

ABOVE **The boxy Pepe crib from Carina's company, xo-in my room, has a simple utilitarian style that makes a strong statement against the decorative mosaic tiles. A colourful net is a neat way to store the toys and books that children like to have at bedtime.**

TOP **Paper plates and drinking straws are everyday accessories in this home, where celebration is a way of life. Traditional paper doilies, an old-fashioned biscuit barrel, a polka-dot teapot and a stack of 1960s pastel cups are the perfect accompaniments for a vintage tea party.**

ABOVE **Family shoes go toe-to-toe on the artificial grass used as carpet in twelve-year-old Bibi's bedroom.**

ABOVE **Sabien and Jan value the importance of family time spent in the fresh air. When they want some freedom, they all head off with their beloved 1964 Yvonne Mostard caravan.**

OPPOSITE **Sabien found two almost identical vintage lockers in different places at different times and lovingly restored them with peacock-blue gloss paint. Cardboard boxes on top of the lockers store important things out of harm's way. A collection of magnets turns the tall, vertical radiator into a noticeboard and a home for photos and drawings.**

FESTIVAL FERVOUR

SABIEN ENGELENBERG AND JAN RIJNVELD TRADED IN THEIR APARTMENT IN THE FASHIONABLE JORDAAN DISTRICT OF AMSTERDAM FOR A CONTEMPORARY SPACE WITHIN A CHILD-FRIENDLY COMMUNITY. THEIR NEW HOME, WHERE THEY LIVE WITH DAUGHTERS BIBI, AGED TWELVE, AND EIGHT-YEAR-OLD MIJNTJE, IS IN A RECENTLY DEVELOPED NEIGHBOURHOOD THAT BUSTLES WITH SMALL FAMILIES AND CREATIVE ENTERPRISES.

The striking use of colour in this home is testament to Sabien's belief that colour makes her feel happy and complete. The hall is covered with vivid examples of children's art, which set the tone for a home where creativity is encouraged to flourish. Strings of brightly coloured bunting festoon the living space and seem to express the notion that every day is worth celebrating.

Sabien's workspace on the ground floor is deliberately isolated from the rest of the house, but still provides an opportunity for a typically bold statement with colour. A yellow 1950s kitchen table adds to the impact of the acid-yellow walls. The Formica tabletop is where Sabien displays her current sources of inspiration.

An open staircase leads to an uplifting living space on the first floor, where the decisive use of colour and print establishes clear divisions. In the kitchen area, a large wooden trestle table and two vintage glass-fronted lockers take centre stage. This is where the family spends most of its time together. Piled high with table- and partyware, one of the lockers defines this as a dining area. The other, stacked with games, paints and sketchbooks, redefines the same space as a well-stocked art room.

One end of the living space is lined with simple white kitchen units and a deep work surface. Pots and pans hang

OPPOSITE **A string of confetti bunting made from discs of printed paper punctuates the length of the living space with flashes of colour and graphic pattern. An oversized latticework paper lampshade on a bright blue flex/cord hangs over the table.**

ABOVE **Fresh flowers add to the ambience and the vitality of the living space, and honour the passing seasons. Sabien buys a single large branch of magnolia each year to celebrate the coming of spring. A group of collectible 1960s German ceramic vases makes a bold addition to the dining table.**

BIBI SAYS "It looks like the whole room is yellow but it is just one wall. The colour makes me really happy. It always feels like the sun is shining."

in happy chaos above the window next to a kitsch plastic garland. Shelves of cookery books are ready and waiting, inviting the girls to bake – an activity they love to share. The space can switch easily from a place for culinary creativity to one for aspiring artists who delight in mixing their own paints.

At the opposite end of the open-plan space, the living area leads to a balcony that overlooks the water and modern skyline. In the summer months, Bibi and Mijntje like to drag the giant floor cushions outside and take it in turns to lie in the hammock. Sabien chose to cover one wall in vintage patterned wallpaper to add visual interest. Hanging on the wall behind the sofa, the

MIJNTJE SAYS "I like the pompoms in my room because I can watch them when I am in my bed. I play games with them by counting them or I try to make words with the same amount of letters."

ABOVE **Sabien has an office hidden away downstairs where she tries to keep her work separate from family life, but she has created such an inspiring space that the girls like to spend time in it, too. Floating wooden cubes hang on the wall and act as neat storage units for sourcebooks and files of paperwork.**

RIGHT **Mijntje likes to line up her favourite things on the bed surround and hide things behind the sliding doors, just as Sabien used to when she was a child. The bed is set on castors and can be pushed away under the unit, transforming it into a sofa and a cosy spot to play with her friends.**

OPPOSITE **The girls always have creative projects on the go. Sabien recently taught them how to knit, using big wooden needles and rolls of colourful, thick, textured yarn. They often get absorbed and forget the time, but a traditional cuckoo clock sings out every hour to keep them on track. The wooden log side table was made especially for Sabien by a friend who lives near a forest.**

BELOW **Tucked around a corner in Mijntje's room, two pairs of mismatched desks and stools are at the ready for play. With a spark of imagination, the space can be transformed into a classroom or a post office. Alternatively, her collection of musical instruments becomes an improvised orchestra. A string of fairy lights has been transformed into colourful lanterns by covering each bulb with paper party cups in scraps of assorted fabrics.**

RIGHT **A reused vintage children's book makes a kitsch and quirky base for a set of bedroom hooks. A collection of necklaces hangs alongside Mijntje's heart-shaped purse and her favourite little bag.**

vibrant pink and orange design she chose gives the area an alluring rosy glow that is picked out by a bold red apple screen-print that hangs nearby.

The open stairs to the second floor lead to the girls' bedrooms. When Sabien found a vintage bed just like the one she used to sleep in at her grandmother's house, she couldn't resist buying it for Mijntje. She can remember the excitement of hiding her treasures in the little compartments behind sliding doors, and her daughter is equally thrilled with it. A wooden armoire originally from Sabien's childhood home has been given a new lease of life with bright pink paint. It sits happily beside zingy yellow and orange vintage wallpaper. A rail of dressing-up clothes provides inspiration for imaginative games.

Bibi's room overlooks the water and has a more grown-up air. A patch of artificial grass adds a note of quirky

BIBI SAYS "I painted the bed with my Auntie Lyke. It came from France. It was a lot of work; every time I touched the bed with my hands I had to paint it again. I chose the colour because it is a mixture of blue and green."

THIS PAGE **Bibi has chosen colours and accessories to stamp her own personality onto her bedroom. Her clever and original idea of using artificial grass instead of a rug reflects her creative upbringing and expresses the sense of joy that she takes in her surroundings. A row of woven plastic baskets underneath the bed makes organizing her things fun.**

FIRST AID

humour, while the old-fashioned, wrought-iron bed has been painted in her favourite shade of green. An orderly desk with pendant lamps provides plenty of well-lit space for homework or art projects. Custom-built floor-to-ceiling wardrobes/closets make the perfect pinboard for posters and drawings, as well as offering lots of clothes storage.

At the top of the house, the master bedroom is flooded with daylight. The room is small but perfectly formed and opens out onto another balcony – a place for Sabien and Jan to call their own once the children have gone to bed. In summer, it is also a magical setting for family picnics.

By definition, a home is a settled and permanent place, but for many families that all too often results in the living space becoming stagnant. Sabien and Jan have the gift of making their home feel spontaneous and open to change, even though every feature of it is unmistakably stamped with their own identity. Living moment by moment and responding to new inspirations mean that everything is graced with the lightest of touches. Moving through this home is like strolling from one tent to another at a festival, where the key to the vibe is not admiring a finished artefact but joining in with a work in progress.

OPPOSITE **The word "LOVE", boldly spelled out in strips of colourful Washi tape, is a heartfelt message on the wall behind Sabien and Jan's bed.**

THIS PAGE **Sabien made paper cherry blossoms out of printed images, then added them to a photographic decal of a tree. A carved block of wood at the base of the tree introduces a natural element into the bedroom.**

MUNTJE SAYS "I like my parents' bedroom. I like to sleep in this room, but not when I am alone because there are a lot of spiders."

URBAN HUB

WHEN LOUISE AND JACOB RIISING WANTED TO MAKE A CHANGE TO THEIR HOME ENVIRONMENT, THEY CAME TO AN UNORTHODOX DECISION. FROM THE IDYLLIC SETTING OF A LARGE HOUSE BY A LAKE, THEY RELOCATED TO THE HEART OF COPENHAGEN ALONG WITH CARLO, AGED EIGHT, SIX-YEAR-OLD MARVIN AND ONE-YEAR-OLD LYKKE, IN SEARCH OF A MORE DYNAMIC URBAN VIBE.

ABOVE RIGHT **Family photos, cards and children's artworks are stuck to a wall, evoking a strong family narrative.**

RIGHT **A collection of pebbles has become a bunch of colourful characters.**

BELOW RIGHT **A lobby lined with box seats provides ample storage for shoes and other outdoor kit.**

Louise and Jacob found a vast city-centre warehouse dating from 1784, which gave them all the space they needed to create a distinctively modern family home. They tore down walls to get rid of narrow corridors and maximize the main living area. The thick industrial walls give the place an air of strength and solidity, while the deep windowsills make natural shelves for books and toys.

Upon entering, the vast living space stretches out in front of you, with dedicated zones for all kinds of exciting activities. In one corner, a fabric-covered wigwam doubles as a walk-in wardrobe/closet for dressing-up games. A round African rug

THIS PAGE **A string of colourful festoon lights turns part of the open-plan living space into a children's circus. The well-worn wooden chairs become ringside seats to watch aerial acrobatics on the round swing.**

CARLO SAYS "If I'm bored, I just take a ride in the swing – that always helps me to come up with a good idea about what to play."

LEFT **Open shelves in the kitchen add a stripe of colour to the white wall. Framed pictures and children's clay models mingle with cooking utensils and kitchen paraphernalia.**

BELOW **A brilliant idea for bringing light into Louise's office and connecting it with the rest of the house was to knock through the wall and put in an exterior-style window.**

adds texture and warmth, and delineates the centre of another play area. Positioned above it, a round swing can accommodate more than one child and has ample space around it for other games. It was a birthday present for Marvin when he was a baby and remains a big hit with all of the children. They use it every day, whether they are having a raucous swing or just taking it easy with a book.

Simple white walls and a grey-painted floor form a neutral backdrop for flashes of vivid colour in the form of children's paintings and toys. When Louise and Jacob went looking for family-friendly art, they found the print called "Cats In Hats" by Stine Maria Aalykke, which they instinctively knew would work in their home. It now hangs in the main living space.

Stylish design pieces are positioned alongside practical items of furniture that work hard for all the family. The status of the IKEA sofa, whose covers can be stripped off and washed whenever necessary, is elevated by being partnered with a wall light from Paolo Rizzatto – a design classic of the future. Louise's home-made floor cushions introduce some Eastern spirit and an ethnic flavour to the home, as well as providing an opportunity for inventive play.

After Louise had painted the interior white and grey, the couple felt that there was a distinct lack of natural materials. They decided to introduce some wooden pieces into the home to warm up the

ABOVE **In the music corner, Jacob and Carlo like to bash away at the electric keyboard, making noisy but rapid progress. There is also a collection of old percussion instruments, so Lykke can join in when she's in the mood.**

space and create a more organic feel. Out went the white dining table and in came a large, wooden trestle table. This has a sturdy, rustic character, which heightens the impact of the sleek, fluid Panton chairs that surround it.

The different types of lighting throughout the space create diverse moods, ranging from the haunting and ethereal to the snug and intimate. Pieces from Louise and Jacob's favourite Danish lighting design house, Design By Us, have been deftly worked into the space. The acrylic Papillon lamp above the dining-room table has a 1960s feel that strikes up a hip rapport with the Panton chairs.

The long galley kitchen provides ample space for preparing meals and also inspires the children to learn to cook and bake. It is a hive of activity at mealtimes. A modern wood-burning stove has been installed in the old chimney stack, and the awkward empty space beside it is filled with a dramatic column of stacked firewood.

MARVIN SAYS "We play 'the earth is poison' on the couch, pillows and other things on the floor."

THIS PAGE **The large Chinese cupboard hides away the family mess, such as books, toys, DVDs and all those things you don't want to have on permanent display in your living room. A plain white wall is given a harlequin twist with simple decals that don't overpower the calm ambience.**

THIS PAGE **A shelf runs along a wall in the living space, creating a temporary gallery and library. Children's art is propped up or simply stuck to the wall. Books of the moment are kept on display to encourage the children to read. Jacob plundered the children's Lego to make the love token for Louise, seen bottom right.**

MARVIN SAYS "Today I took all the pillows in the house and transformed my bedroom into a huge Lounge so it's ready for a movie tonight when Carlo comes home."

For the time being, Carlo and Marvin love sharing a bedroom and retreat there to play, watch movies or to hatch plans. There isn't a hint of gender stereotyping here, as spotlights, cushions and a sunshine-yellow cupboard bring colour and cheer to their space. A Perspex unit hanging on the wall beside the bunk beds is home to the brothers' assorted treasures.

Lykke currently sleeps in a cot/crib in the charmed atmosphere of her parents' bedroom. Here, the sylvan-patterned wallpaper creates a calm and tranquil atmosphere that is balanced by a whimsical cloud mobile that sways gently in the breeze.

This is a home that manages to combine hipster cool and minimalist designs with a cosy and relaxed family environment – no mean feat. Louise and Jacob possess an aesthetic vision that offers an innovative take on contemporary minimalist design, resulting in an atmosphere of easy-going generosity and charm.

ABOVE **Bunk beds are not just for sleeping in – they inspire children to play all sorts of inventive games. Here, in Carlo and Marvin's bedroom, a pair of tiger-printed binoculars is all ready for a safari adventure.**

LEFT **A single wall with an enchanted arboreal repeat print bestows a calm atmosphere in the master bedroom. Dip-dyed bedding combines a graduated burst of intense coral with a contrasting grid design. The elegant upholstered bedhead is unusually tall and places the focus firmly on the bed.**

WOLF SAYS "I really like the chickens in our garden. Did you know they are related to dinosaurs? You can tell by their feet. They look the same as the feet of the Tyrannosaurus Rex!"

THIS PAGE **A kaleidoscope of colour and pattern turns the dining room into a visual feast. A carefully chosen selection of seating has something for everyone: the ubiquitous Tripp Trapp chair for Mus, the versatile bench seat for Wolf and retro-style chairs for the grown-ups.**

OPPOSITE ABOVE LEFT **You won't find any gender stereotyping in this home – the boys love the floral-printed tableware.**

We hebben deze foto's ook allemaal digitaal ergens... Casper weet wel waar van.

de landcamera is wel erg leuk, maar de foto's zijn kwalitatief niet goed genoeg, vindt U.

April 2011, met de landcamera.
Het was erg warm deze maand. Wolf speelde veel buiten met water. Het was de maand waarin we Mus eigenlijk verwachtten.
Het wereldnieuws ging vooral over de kernramp in Japan, daar hebben papa & mama zich ook best druk om gemaakt. Uiteindelijk zou het voor Nederland geen gevaar betekenen - zeggen ze

BELOW **A collection of well-worn, multi-coloured sneakers. This is one family you can't imagine in run-of-the-mill footwear.**

ABOVE Anki keeps a visual diary where she sticks Polaroids with colourful Washi tape. She treasures memories of the boys' childhood and includes funny little anecdotes and quotes in her book. When the boys are older, they will have great fun reading through them.

PLAYFUL PALETTE

SURROUNDED BY FORESTS AND FENLAND IN A SMALL TOWN OUTSIDE AMSTERDAM, ANKI WIJNEN AND CASPER BOOT HAVE CREATED A PLAYFUL HOME FOR THEIR TWO BOYS: WOLF, AGED SIX, AND ONE-YEAR-OLD MUS. THEIR MANTRA – "NEVER GROW UP" – IS PROCLAIMED ON A SCREEN-PRINTED POSTER OF THEIR OWN DESIGN. EVERYTHING YOU ENCOUNTER IN THIS HOME IS A REMINDER THAT AGE IS SIMPLY A STATE OF MIND.

ABOVE **A Smeg fridge was the first purchase for their home and has proved to be the signature piece that marked the beginning of Anki and Casper's joint exploration of colour. Wolf was upset when he discovered at school that boys were not supposed to like pink. It was a good opportunity to tell him that it's OK to be yourself and to stand out from the crowd.**

ABOVE RIGHT **White shelves are a simple platform for lovingly arranged displays that change frequently with the seasons. Neat little piles of books are wrapped up together with strips of paper to create maverick anthologies.**

When Anki and Casper moved into this traditional 1930s house, they immediately set about knocking down walls and adding an extension with a glass roof. They wanted to create a unified living space where they could spend time together as a family.

The white walls on the ground floor provide a simple backdrop that the couple have layered with colour, print and pattern, to create a home that celebrates the best of modern design. The dining room and kitchen are enlivened by black-and-white floor tiles, which are in stark contrast to the vibrant colours elsewhere. In the kitchen, pastel shades of pink and blue provide a change of mood from the tangy pops of red and lime in the dining area next door.

Anki and Casper had a vision of a home with a strong heart and went to great lengths and great expense to install a chimney so that they could have the wood burner of their dreams – a Dutch Stonestove. When lit, it exudes warmth and comfort and becomes a focal point, drawing the family together.

OPPOSITE **A red kettle asks the pertinent question "Why should I be white?" The Pinocchio funnel hanging above it is the perfect example of practicality with a playful twist, while the dishwasher has been given humorous eyes and a tongue. A bird decal perches atop the back door, enlivening an otherwise empty space.**

WOLF SAYS "Our dishwasher is a plate-washing monster! My friends' houses are boring. Everything is so the same, it's dull. There are no funny things, or bright colours."

THIS PAGE **Mus loves to stand at the window and watch the trains passing by on the track across the road. The deep sill is a wonderful surface for building with the boys' Kapla wooden blocks. Cities and rockets stand tall until it's decided they need rebuilding.**

THIS PAGE **Give a child a defined space
that you are happy for them to draw on,
and add a box of chalks. They will then
create something unique that can bring
a piece of furniture to life. The pictures
chalked on this bold red cupboard
capture the children's creativity
and make it part of the aesthetic
of their home.**

RIGHT AND BELOW **Themes and interests that are important to the family are recurring visual motifs throughout the home. The forest wallpaper in Mus's room (below) pays homage to the couple's passion for wildlife and to Casper's voluntary work as a forest guide. The brightly painted orange wall is echoed in the vibrant orange-painted bookshelf and the top-stitching on a colourful patchwork crocheted blanket (right).**

Everything in this home combines fun and function. Anki and Casper are both self-confessed kids at heart and share a childlike sense of humour. They seek to bring wonder into everyday life and have filled their home with objects that are both unusual and unexpected. Philippe Starck's moulded-plastic gnome tables and the Ron Arad Bookworm shelf epitomize their playful style. These things appeal to the children as much as they do to

the adults, and there is a shared joy in the choices they have made. Deciding on a new sofa was the perfect example of Casper and Anki's approach to family living. They chose colourful modular seating by Kartell that is fun for the boys to play on and has the advantage of being easy to clean. If they need to increase the number of seats, they can simply buy an additional unit.

The lighting choices demonstrate a broad stylistic spectrum. A Jieldé lamp attached to the ceiling illuminates the main living space, while an oversized fabric lampshade with a vintage feel hangs over the dining-room table. A Normann Copenhagen Norm 69 lampshade adds frivolity to the kitchen, and a transparent Fly light in pink introduces yet another colour to the living room.

WOLF SAYS "We have the coolest home and I sleep the highest, right up in the attic — that's the best!"

THIS PAGE **Given a free rein, Wolf says he would have painted the floor and the walls in his room black. After discussing less-extreme options with Anki and Casper, he ultimately chose owl- and forest-printed wallpaper. This still has a sombre resonance, but rather than feeling lost in the depths of the forest, the room has become a dappled clearing in the trees.**

There is an eclectic mix of storage to be found here. A set of white, child-sized wooden lockers, rescued from a boarding school, is home to tableware, paints and board games. A Rococo-style chest of drawers, enhanced by delicate pink paint, introduces an element of kitsch, and an old-fashioned wooden cupboard has been given a new lease of life with a coat of pillarbox-red gloss paint.

Upstairs, the house becomes narrower and the walls slope inwards, creating the feeling that the attic is a completely separate zone. Mus's bedroom conjures up a dream-like sylvan mood with a photographic forest wallpaper. An old wardrobe/closet bought from Marktplatz (the Dutch eBay) has been transformed into an uplifting piece of furniture with thick layers of vibrant-yellow paint.

Behind a sliding door in Anki and Casper's bedroom, instead of an en-suite bathroom or walk-in wardrobe/closet, a small home office offers solitude. Tucked away like an ante-chamber, the quiet of the space is only disturbed by the cooing of birds as they peck at the feeder outside.

At the top of a steep flight of stairs, Wolf's attic bedroom is shaped by sharply sloping eaves that conjure up images of camping beneath the stars, of teepees and golden eagles. This is a great place for imaginary play and for venturing into the land of dreams.

Anki and Casper have a very clear idea of their ideal family home. They have a wishlist of modern designs that mesh with their vision and they save up until they can afford to buy them, piece by piece. However, these objects aren't purchased and displayed with a consumerist mindset. Instead, they are played with, joyously reinvented and embraced in the life of the family, in a spirit that says "Never Grow Up".

ABOVE **An assortment of handmade furnishings works with the printed wallpaper to create a rich medley of textures and patterns in the master bedroom. Space is maximized with valuable storage under the bed. A fluorescent pink tube light leans at an angle against the sloping eaves and throws out a rosy glow after dark.**

OPPOSITE **The classic Uten.Silo organizer belonged to Anki when she was a child, but she gave it away to a neighbour who looked after it for over 20 years. With the passage of time, it has acquired iconic status and has resumed its central position in her adult life.**

SHIP SHAPE

CAMILLA AND ANDREAS'S MODERN MINIMALIST HOME IS IN THE OLD INDUSTRIAL HARBOUR OF COPENHAGEN. WITHIN WALKING DISTANCE OF THE SEA AND SURROUNDED BY CANALS, THEY HAVE NURTURED THEIR FOUR-YEAR-OLD SON SIGURD'S CONNECTION WITH NATURE AND HIS AFFINITY WITH WATER. BY COMBINING THE MASS-PRODUCED AND THE HANDCRAFTED, THE COUPLE HAVE COME UP WITH INNOVATIVE AND UNPRETENTIOUS STYLING IDEAS FOR THEIR FAMILY HOME.

Behind the nondescript front door of this waterside home lies a delightful and unexpected surprise: a double-height cuboid space flooded with natural light. Views of sky above and water below elevate the spirit and make this an uplifting place in which to live. A subtle and considered sailing theme runs through this home, giving it a distinctive stylistic motif and a light-hearted twist. The collection of nautical artefacts affirms the relationship between the home and its immediate environment.

The presence of the canal outside is highlighted by the vast floor-to-ceiling windows and by the way the water comes right up to the wooden deck. Sigurd can

ABOVE **A medley of family photographs and memorabilia is pinned to a framed noticeboard, together with drawings and scribbles.**

ABOVE **Vintage egg-cups give breakfast a quirky seafaring flavour.**

LEFT **Wellies are at the ready for a country walk. Low hooks allow Sigurd to hang up his own coat.**

SIGURD SAYS "I'm looking forward to when it's summer and warm. Then we go down to the water and jump in."

THIS PAGE A porthole painting left over from Sigurd's sailor-themed party remains stuck to the kitchen cupboard, where it has become a stylistic keynote. Sigurd was given free rein to decorate a basic wooden IKEA stool with his own paints and turned it into a colourful piece of furniture.

play on the small bridges that cross over the network of canals and use his fishing net to catch small fish and crabs. On rainy days, the family likes to take the water bus close to their home into Copenhagen for gallery and museum visits.

In the living area, the minimalist aesthetic of the modern sofa is softened by neat piles of whimsical cushions. During the day, this split-level space doubles up as an exciting indoor playground. A colourful playhouse from Lucky Boy Sunday is the most imaginative of dens. It can be moved around the space to become a cabin on board ship or a cave on a desert island, while the rope swing hanging from the mezzanine is a versatile prop for Sigurd's games.

A tidy kitchen flanks two sides of the double-height living area. Above the cabinets, there is plenty of space to display or store objects that might otherwise be damaged by Sigurd's football. A treasure trove of vintage finds is displayed in wooden boxes, creating layers of interest and intrigue, like cargo on a quayside. Burnished copper pans hang from an old ladder, imparting soul and character to the kitchen area. An iconic Kay Bojesen Monkey hangs from one of the metal cabinet handles in the kitchen – an example of classic Danish design that is destined to be handed down through the generations.

ABOVE **The dining area is sparse, but the exquisite choice of contrasting materials and shapes evokes a sense of serenity. Sleek stainless steel and chunky burnished wood are offset by green foliage and the reflections of the water outside.**

OPPOSITE **Inspired by tales of pirates, Sigurd loves the rope swing that hangs from the mezzanine. It encourages imaginary play and is a great way for him to burn off surplus energy.**

SIGURD SAYS "I can do different tricks with the rope — swing and jump and land like a Ninja."

The simple wooden dining table sits in a corner overlooking the canal. Camilla and Andreas chose a piece of wood in a workshop on a plantation in Bali for the tabletop and had it shipped home. It is a celebration of traditional craftsmanship and ethical production, values that they both hold in great esteem. The iconic Charles Eames fibreglass chairs are a brilliant contrast with the natural materials of the table. The reproduction arc lamp provides the perfect source of light at mealtimes and for art sessions or board games. The classic Tripp Trapp chair in ultramarine adds a splash of colour to the space and recalls the nautical ambience that prevails elsewhere.

CROWN

India

POLITIKENS STORE VERDENS ATLAS

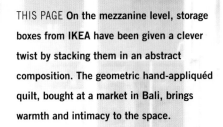

THIS PAGE **On the mezzanine level, storage boxes from IKEA have been given a clever twist by stacking them in an abstract composition. The geometric hand-appliquéd quilt, bought at a market in Bali, brings warmth and intimacy to the space.**

THIS PAGE **There is a friendly quality to the hippo poster, the clown light and the collection of ceramic ghosts that keep Sigurd company in his bedroom. An assortment of cushions and blankets makes his bedroom snug and cosy.**

HAVE

SIGURD SAYS "Sometimes I'm Captain Hook and have a hook and patch for my eye - the hook is really sharp!"

Entering the mezzanine space is rather like walking a narrow gangplank, but with the reward of a cosy bed at the end of it. Like the crow's nest of a galleon, it looks down over the living space and is a great spot for playing pirates. The family enjoys spending time in this hideout, watching movies or reading stories.

Along the corridor, Sigurd's room is the starting point for a world of fun and action-packed adventure. Animal masks, superhero costumes, swords and pirate flags all hang on the wall ready for playtime. Having the bed on the floor makes the room feel more spacious and means there is plenty of extra height when it is used for a particularly energetic trampoline session. Sigurd likes to stick his favourite posters up on his bedroom wall wherever he wants to. You can imagine him playing imaginary games inspired by the different characters and doing battle with the rhino on the poster from Copenhagen Zoo.

This home is a lesson in how to capitalize on a truly inspirational location, but the light touch and droll sense of humour mean that you never feel the house is showing off.

ABOVE TOP LEFT AND BELOW LEFT **Tiny vintage toys and ornaments collected over time for Sigurd are gathered together in an intriguing miscellany. A Jolly Roger, lashed to a branch picked up on a forest walk, grins from the bedroom wall.**

ABOVE RIGHT **Being close to water has a calming influence on children. The deck is a tranquil place to sit and watch the ducks and boats float by.**

SEAGULL SKIES

MASCHA VAN REIZEN MOVED TO HAARLEM, OUTSIDE AMSTERDAM, WHEN SHE WAS A STUDENT IN SEARCH OF LOWER RENTS, MORE SPACE AND SEA AIR. TWENTY YEARS LATER, SHE IS STILL THERE AND HAS CREATED A HAPPY AND SAFE HAVEN IN A TRADITIONAL 1930S DUTCH HOUSE WITH HER PARTNER JURGEN TIJMS AND SIX-YEAR-OLD BRITT.

BRITT SAYS "I love the light and space in our house. With nice weather we open the doors and live outside."

LEFT **An exquisite arrangement of delicate branches and magnolia buds decorated with favourite photographs is a resourceful alternative to a family tree. Simple paper prints have a fragile quality, creating a naive charm.**

LEFT **Red shoes make a confident statement shared by Mascha and her daughter, while Jurgen's utilitarian high tops are a classic emblem of rock-solid dependability.**

RIGHT **An asymmetrical arrangement of plates adorns the the blue wall leading to the dining room.**

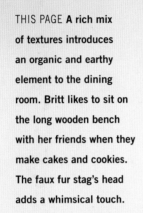

THIS PAGE **A rich mix of textures introduces an organic and earthy element to the dining room. Britt likes to sit on the long wooden bench with her friends when they make cakes and cookies. The faux fur stag's head adds a whimsical touch.**

THIS PAGE **Floor-to-ceiling French** windows allow the dining room to be filled with natural light and also appear to lengthen the room by blurring the division between indoors and out. The lollipop topiary trees in giant plant pots on the deck have a storybook quality about them that appeals to children.

ABOVE **Britt uses the bright yellow stool in the kitchen to stand at the counter when she helps with baking and cooking. When she and her friends are playing on the deck, they can wander in and out to get their own drinks.**

Arriving at Mascha and Jurgen's seaside home, with seagulls flying overhead, there is a tranquil and relaxed atmosphere. Behind a door from the street, a steep flight of stairs leads up to a large decked terrace and a home that is above street level and nestled neatly behind a row of houses, creating the feeling of a secluded hideaway.

This broad terrace is Britt's playground, where she stages imaginary games that revolve around her wooden playhouse and the artificial grass lawn. Brightly coloured garden furniture defines the space as an outside room, with low-level lounge seating and an area for alfresco dining. Large French windows from the dining room and the glass door to the kitchen both open out onto the terrace, creating a free flow of space and energy around the home.

The kitchen is light and functional, with elements of print and pattern that lift the white space and lend

THIS PAGE **A large plastic woven rug brings texture to bare boards while being immensely practical. When it needs to be cleaned, it can be simply wiped or hosed down on the terrace. The glass table offers a flat, smooth surface for Britt to paint on and is also easy to clean.**

BRITT SAYS "When I close the sliding doors, this room is mine. Then I can dance, play and paint. No grown-ups are allowed!"

it plenty of zest. Mascha wanted to give Britt a wall that she could draw on and where they could write their weekly shopping lists, so she covered one of the kitchen walls in washable whiteboard paint. This playful space features writing and drawings that hint at the child-friendly home beyond.

The adjoining dining room has a cheerful, informal atmosphere. A long glass table is teamed with a bench made from reclaimed wood, white moulded-plastic seats and an old machinist's chair. Three lengths of pictorial wallpaper, each in a different colourway but from the same series, hang behind the table. Spaced at regular intervals, they do not dominate the space but instead introduce colour and detail. A stag's head on the wall, rescued from a flower shop that was closing down, continues the theme.

Art Deco stained-glass sliding doors separate the living room from the dining room and can be pulled across when Britt wants to play secret games. In here, simple modular sofas with piles of colourful cushions offer versatile seating and are great for lounging and playing. Art materials are kept at the ready in a low-level filing cabinet. They are stored in supermarket-style wire baskets that are great for carrying from room to room whenever inspiration strikes.

ABOVE **Mass-produced canvases have become affordable and are readily available. They make children's pictures long-lasting and more special. Here, sunset colours have created a vibrant piece of art that Britt calls "Fantasy Painting". It's a variation of abstract painting that she has been taught at school.**

RIGHT **Child-sized spaces are great fun to play in, and the old fireplace, with Britt's favourite books, is the perfect little nook for reading. Filled with cushions, it becomes a cosy den. A menagerie of Britt's cut-out animals is ranged along the mantelpiece.**

Britt was very much involved in the colour scheme for her bedroom. By encouraging her to make her own choices, she has turned the room into her own personal world. It's somewhere that she loves to spend time with her friends. A collection of cut-out animal cushions brings the room to life and can double up as toys. A vintage school poster of a polar bear and Britt's collection of plastic deer celebrate her love of animals.

Mascha and Jurgen's bedroom is alive with colour and texture. An array of cushions includes a whimsical tapestry bird that makes reference to the name of their street. Bathed in sunlight, this is a room for relaxation and enjoyment as well as sleep. A sliding door covered in a patchwork of colourful wallpaper samples leads to a huge walk-in wardrobe/closet that keeps the bedroom free of clutter, and the en-suite bathroom gives the room a sense of grown-up opulence.

Up a steep flight of stairs is Britt's room. When they took down the false ceiling in here, Mascha and Jurgen discovered beams and a high ceiling. Stripping the room back to its original architecture gave them an exciting starting point for creating the ultimate child's bedroom. An old-fashioned wooden swing is a magical centrepiece that is a joy to both Britt and her friends. A box seat was custom-built to fit under the window.

ABOVE **A selection of paper lampshades bunched together hangs from coloured cord to shine plenty of light in Britt's attic bedroom. Elements that would normally be found outside make this a magical place. The swing is something that Britt can enjoy either with her friends or when she is on her own. Dressing-up clothes hang on the wooden, tree-shaped coat-stand as instant props for games.**

LEFT **Mascha found this charming, old-fashioned wooden box at a flea market. Letters stamped on pieces of cardboard each have their own compartment that's just the right size for little fingers. Britt loves to sort through them, which encourages her to play spelling games.**

BRITT SAYS "I chose the colour of my bedroom wall myself. It reminds me of the sea and it makes me feel happy."

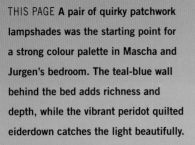

THIS PAGE A pair of quirky patchwork lampshades was the starting point for a strong colour palette in Mascha and Jurgen's bedroom. The teal-blue wall behind the bed adds richness and depth, while the vibrant peridot quilted eiderdown catches the light beautifully.

BRITT SAYS "I really love my two cats Wiki and Mango. Mascha and Jurgen's big bed is a great place to play with them."

LEFT **A redundant old picture frame with broken glass was painted the same colour as the wall and hangs on ribbon that matches the bedspread. The frame has a ledge deep enough to stand little figures or postcards. The white objects are in stark contrast to the teal-blue wall.**

RIGHT **Britt is lucky enough to have her own bathroom, which she shares with guests. The decor is perfect for a young child and brims with optimism. The wood-panelled walls are painted white to contrast with alcoves painted a sunny yellow.**

A thick mattress and piles of cushions make this a cosy place to lounge and read, yet once the cushions are thrown to one side, it becomes a stage for impromptu performances. Pieces of vintage furniture add personality to the room, and a colourful rag rug and felted fake animal skin introduce interesting textures to the painted wooden floor. When Britt is older, the space will be adapted by constructing a bed on a ledge under the eaves.

This is a unique home that mixes the best of the old with the best of the new. Mascha and Jurgen's approach has created an atmosphere of easy-going charm and it's no surprise that this is the favoured place for Britt and her friends to hang out. The relaxed beach-hut ambience plays on the seaside location, but there is also elegance and chic in the mix of 1930s style and contemporary design.

RIGHT **The family treasures its outdoor space and uses it as an additional room. It's an inspiring place for Britt to play independently without being too far away from her parents. During the summer months, they eat their meals outside and enjoy watering the flowers together.**

THIS PAGE **The sturdy and practical coffee table has a Bauhaus feel to it, with bench seats that slot neatly underneath when not in use. The children love to change their routine by eating their meals here or to join in with the favourite family activity of planning the next holiday.**

LILI SAYS "I really like the painting because I know the painter Alicia Omedes and I love the colours."

BELOW **Collecting flamenco shoes for Lili has become a fun family tradition. Her first pair, covered in polka dots, came from an old-fashioned cobbler that Paola discovered on a trip to Seville.**

FAR RIGHT **The children's breakfast bar is adorned with a wooden sign that reads "Chocolat".**

BELOW RIGHT **A photograph of Lili taken by Frank Malthiery for *Vogue Bambini* hangs in an antique frame. Other family pictures are displayed alongside in an eclectic jumble of frames.**

MEDITERRANEAN HEIGHTS

A 1950S PENTHOUSE, WITH VIEWS OVER THE TREETOPS TO THE SEA BEYOND, ACHIEVES A MAGICAL SENSE OF LIVING OUTSIDE THE CITY WHEN ACTUALLY IT IS RIGHT ON TOP OF IT. PAOLA SELLS AND HER HUSBAND GUILLERMO VÁZQUEZ LIVE IN THIS BARCELONA APARTMENT ALONG WITH THEIR CHILDREN GUILLAUME, AGED ELEVEN, AND LILI, AGED EIGHT.

An unusually spacious hall is the highway of this home. It has always been a play space for the children, where they invent games that travel from one room to another. They love to follow their parents around, so the space is shared and used in a very fluid, almost nomadic way.

ABOVE **The roof terrace is a sanctuary on sunny days. A 19th-century wirework dining table and a set of matching chairs, plumped with colourful cushions, create a magical alfresco living space.**

LEFT **Paola has turned an old-fashioned light-fitting into a personalized and idiosyncratic version of a classic chandelier by decorating it with her own handwritten notes and jottings. A collection of cameras and an array of seashells set classic technology and natural forms side by side on the vintage bookcase.**

The focal point of the living space is a huge and dramatic abstract oil painting by a friend, which hangs over the sofa and makes a bold statement. Far from being stuffy or precious, Paola's revered collections are part of the children's world, too, and they are both encouraged to take an interest in their surroundings and the objects that give their home its distinct sense of style.

In the kitchen, a wooden breakfast bar gives Guillaume and Lili somewhere to perch and help with baking and cooking, as well as eat their breakfast or have a quick snack. A strategically placed clock on the wall encourages the children to take charge of their

morning schedules. Giving them responsibility is a simple concept that makes for a smooth-running home. Paola's collection of vintage bowls and dishes is used at every mealtime and are there to be enjoyed, rather than reserved for special occasions.

The children are spoiled for choice when it comes to doing their homework. They tend to gravitate to the dining table, which is surrounded with original 1960s office chairs inherited from their father's grandmother. In this space, broad shelves line the walls from floor to ceiling, and are home to magazines and books, as well as two giant hourglasses, which are used for any game where you

Guillaume's bedroom combines sporty boyish elements with bright splashes of colour and cosy handcrafted furnishings. The poster above the bed by Natalie Lete reinforces the travel theme, adding an element of fantasy. The vivid patterns and colours create a happy and optimistic space that he loves to be in.

SANTA PANCRACIO

GUILLAUME SAYS "I feel very quiet and relaxed when I am in my own bed. I enjoy my own space."

AMÉRIQUE DU NORD

Canada

New-York

END
1
KEY WEST

play against the clock. Tucked around the corner is a compact study area where both parents and children can withdraw to work in peace and quiet. To make the space even more secluded, an antique textile screen can be moved across. A simple floor-length white curtain screens the sun from the French windows that lead out onto a leafy roof terrace. A precious gift on clear days, this tranquil space feels far away from the hustle and bustle on the streets below.

Guillaume is as fascinated by travel as his parents are. Before a family trip to the USA, Paola and Guillermo discovered a vintage map of North America in a flea

LILI SAYS "I'm very happy with my bedroom. I love it even more when it's in order!"

THIS PAGE **Soft colours and floral prints come together to create an enchanting bedroom for Lili. Inherited wooden furniture has been given a new lease of life with a few coats of tea-rose pink paint. The huge mirror on the wardrobe/closet door was replaced with a panel of textured fabric to make it less imposing and more child-friendly.**

LEFT **An old toy kitchen with wooden pots and pans provides hours of fun. An intriguing woodland poster in gorgeous rich colours by Natalie Lete adds a poetic dimension to the play corner, where Lili holds court at tea parties with her dolls.**

RIGHT AND BELOW **At the end of the day, Paola empties the contents of her pockets into a vintage suitcase that has become a repository for the flotsam and jetsam of everyday life. Searching through it, she often finds something to remind her of a long-forgotten day.**

market in France. It has now become a cherished possession and adorns Guillaume's bedroom wall. Growing up with maps and globes fuels a curiosity about faraway lands and has nurtured his instinct to explore the world.

Lili's cosy bedroom is alive with a sense of wonder. A collection of miniature pictures and a vintage handbag that have taken her fancy are pinned to the wall next to her bed. Kitsch rabbit and toadstool night lights bathe the room in a gentle glow at bedtime. Next door, Paola and Guillermo's bedroom is a serene and simple retreat, with bare walls and unobtrusive storage that provides display space for some of Paola's treasured antiques-shop finds.

This home is notable for the way it harmoniously balances Guillermo and Paola's tastes with the needs and interests of the children. Beautiful objects and rare possessions sit alongside more functional pieces. This apartment may be high above the busy city streets, but there's nothing aloof about the down-to-earth ethos of family life as it's lived here.

SOURCES

Cass Arts
www.cassarts.co.uk
+44 (0)20 7354 2999
An emporium for young artists.

Creative Family Home
www.creativefamilyhome.com
Inspiration for creative families.

Ferm Living
www.ferm-living.com
Scandinavian interior products.

Handmade Charlotte
www.handmadecharlotte.com
A blog with DIY craft projects and design inspiration.

Heartwood Burners
www.heartwoodburners.co.uk
Wood-burning stoves and approved installation in the UK.

Kids On Roof
www.kidsonroof.com
Innovative recycled cardboard playhouses and rockets.

Minakani Lab
www.minakanilab.com
Exceptional wallpaper with a bold emphasis on colour.

Mini Moderns
www.minimoderns.co.uk
+44 (0) 207 737 6767
British interior products for design-conscious families

Oh Happy Day
DIY projects and party ideas.

Olive Loves Alfie
84 Stoke Newington Church St
London N16 0AP
+44 (0)207 241 4212

www.olivelovesalfie.co.uk
Ashlyn Gibson's definitive family lifestyle store.

Pappelina
www.pappelina.com
Practical, beautiful rugs made from European environmentally certified plastics.

Retrouvius
www.retrouvius.com
1016 Harrow Road
London NW10 5NS
+44 (0)20 8960 6060
Architectural salvage, mid-century furniture and quirky one-off pieces.

Sunbury Antiques Market
www.sunburyantiques.com
A prop-buyer's favourite for vintage furniture from Europe.

Sitting Spiritually
www.sittingspitually.co.uk
+44 (0)1297 443084
Wooden swings handmade in the UK from FSC-certified sustainable timber.

String
www.string.se
Modular shelving systems.

Surfacephilia
www.surfacephilia.co.uk
+44 (0) 7771 577672
Bohemian patterns for interiors.

tiny & little
www.tinyandlittle.com
A blog that celebrates the joy of the family through stories, activities and photography.

Check out the business credits overleaf for details of the bloggers, designers and stores featured in this book.

PICTURE CREDITS

All photographs by Rachel Whiting.

Endpapers The home of Sabien Engelenburg, the founder/designer of engelpunt.com; **1** The home of Britt, Jurgen and Mascha; **2** The home of Susanne Brandt and her family in Copenhagen; **3** Anki Wijnen & Casper Boot of www.zilverblauw.nl & www.jahallo.nl; **4–5** The home of Britt, Jurgen and Mascha; **5 above inset** Anki Wijnen & Casper Boot of www.zilverblauw.nl & www.jahallo.nl; **5 below inset** The home of Sabien Engelenburg, the founder/designer of engelpunt.com; **6** The home of Sabien Engelenburg, the founder/designer of engelpunt.com; **7** The home of Susanne Brandt and her family in Copenhagen; **7 left inset** Anki Wijnen & Casper Boot of www.zilverblauw.nl & www.jahallo.nl; **7 centre and right insets** The home of Britt, Jurgen and Mascha; **8** The family home of Louise Kamman Riising, co-owner of hey-home.dk; **9** Anki Wijnen & Casper Boot of www.zilverblauw.nl & www.jahallo.nl; **10** The family home of Camilla Ebdrup of LUCKYBOYSUNDAY; **11 above left** The home of Susanne Brandt and her family in Copenhagen; **11 above right** The home of Britt, Jurgen and Mascha; **11 below** The home of the Ponsa-Hemmings family of xo-inmyroom.com; **12 above** The home of Ashlyn Gibson, founder of children's concept store Olive Loves Alfie, interior stylist/writer and children's fashion stylist; **12 below** The family home of Louise and Garth Jennings in London; **13 above left** The home of Nadine Richter, designer and co-owner of Noé & Zoë in Berlin; **13 above right** The family home of Louise and Garth Jennings in London; **13 below right** Anki Wijnen & Casper Boot of www.zilverblauw.nl & www.jahallo.nl; **14 above** The home of Britt, Jurgen and Mascha; **14 centre** The home of Sabien Engelenburg, the founder/designer of engelpunt.com; **14 below** The home of Nici Zinell, designer of Noé & Zoë in Berlin, and Knut Hake, film editor; **15** The home of Susanne Brandt and her family in Copenhagen; **16 above left** The family home of Louise Kamman Riising, co-owner of hey-home.dk; **16 above right** The home of Ashlyn Gibson, founder of children's concept store Olive Loves Alfie, interior stylist/writer and children's fashion stylist; **16 centre right** Anki Wijnen & Casper Boot of www.zilverblauw.nl & www.jahallo.nl; **16 below and 17 above** The home of Nici Zinell, designer of Noé & Zoë in Berlin, and Knut Hake, film editor; **17 below** The home of Susanne Brandt and her family in Copenhagen; **18 above left** Anki Wijnen & Casper Boot of www.zilverblauw.nl & www.jahallo.nl; **18 above centre** The family home of Camilla Ebdrup of LUCKYBOYSUNDAY; **18 above right** The family home of Paola Sells of www.sugarkids.es in Barcelona; **18 below left** The home of Britt, Jurgen and Mascha; **18 below right and 19 above** The home of Susanne Brandt and her family in Copenhagen; **19 below** The family home of Louise and Garth Jennings in London; **20 left** The home of Nici Zinell, designer of Noé & Zoë in Berlin, and Knut Hake, film editor; **20 right** The home of the Ponsa-Hemmings family of xo-inmyroom.com; **21** The family

BUSINESS CREDITS

Anki Wijnen
www.zilverblauw.nl
and
Casper Boot
www.jahallo.nl
Pages 3, 5 above inset, 7 left inset, 9, 12 below, 16 centre right, 18 above left, 22, 122–131.

Ashlyn Gibson
www.ashlyngibson.co.uk
www.creativefamilyhome.com
Olive Loves Alfie
84 Stoke Newington
 Church Street
London N16 0AP
T: +44 (0)20 7241 4212
www.oliveloves alfie.co.uk
Pages 12 above, 16 above right, 25–26, 36 below, 37 below, 40 centre left, 44–53.

Camilla Ebdrup
www.luckyboysunday.dk
Pages 10, 18 above centre, 31 above left, 37 above, 132–139.

Carina Hemmings
www.shop.xo-inmyroom.com
Pages 11 below, 20 right, 32 above centre, 34 below, 96–113.

Fons Cohen and Katja de Jong
Imps&Elfs
Head office and store
Sloterkade 41–44
1058 HE Amsterdam
The Netherlands
T: +31 (0)20 346 0201
www.imps-elfs.nl
Pages 39 above, 64–69.

Louise Kamman Riising
www.hey-home.dk
Pages 8, 16 above left, 23 left, 31 above, 31 below left, 114–121.

Nadine Richter and Nici Zinell
Noé & Zoë
Berlin
T: +49 1736843736
E: info@noe-zoe.com
www.noe-zoe.com
Pages 13 above left, 14 below, 16 below, 17 above, 20 left, 24 above left, 27 below, 28 below, 31, 33 left, 34 above left, 34–35 above, 35 below right, 39 below left, 54–63, 88–95, 160.

Paola Sells
www.sugarkids.es
Pages 18 above right, 21, 29 below, 40 below left, 150–155.

Sabien Engelenburg
ENGEL.
www.engelpunt.com
"Life is a party but it is your job to hang out the bunting!"
Pages endpapers, 5 below inset, 6 inset, 14 centre, 23 above right, 29 above, 30 above, 32 below right, 33 right, 36 above, 38 above left, 42–53.

INDEX

ACKNOWLEDGMENTS

Thank you to Elizabeth Machin, my wonderful PR, for her belief in my vision and for introducing me to the dynamic team at Ryland Peters & Small. Thanks also to Rachel Whiting, my compadre, for her dedication and for her inspiring photographs, and to Joe Morris for his generosity in completing the title font used in this book. I am indebted to all the home owners, who trusted me with the intimacy of their family lives, and to their children, who brighten the world with their creativity.

Thank you to Donna Powell for keeping the ball rolling at Olive Loves Alfie, to to my dad Roland Gibson for inspiring me with his love of vintage style, and to my mum Mavis Gulliver for her loving guidance and for filling my childhood with creativity. Thanks to Matthew Lloyd, my love and best friend, for his boundless support and encouragement. And to Olive, my daughter, whose uniqueness inspires me every day.

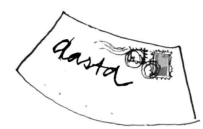

To my own Bjorn.

BLOOMSBURY
CHILDREN'S
BOOKS

First published in Great Britain in 1999
by Bloomsbury Publishing PLC
38 Soho Square, London, W1V 5DF

Text and illustrations copyright © Stina Langlo Ørdal 1999

A CIP catalogue record of this book is available from the
British Library

ISBN 0 7475 4127 2

Printed and bound in Hong Kong by South China Printing Co.

1 3 5 7 9 10 8 6 4 2

Princess Aasta

Stina Langlo Ørdal

BLOOMSBURY
CHILDREN'S
BOOKS

Once upon a time

there was a little princess

called **Aasta,**

who wanted a bear

to love.

She decided to send a letter to a newspaper – "Little princess seeking big, cuddly bear friend".

Shortly afterwards, she received letters from bears all over the world.

Black, brown and white **bears,** and even **grizzly bears.**

Princess Aasta was **very** **excited** and went through

all the letters,

(there were many of them).

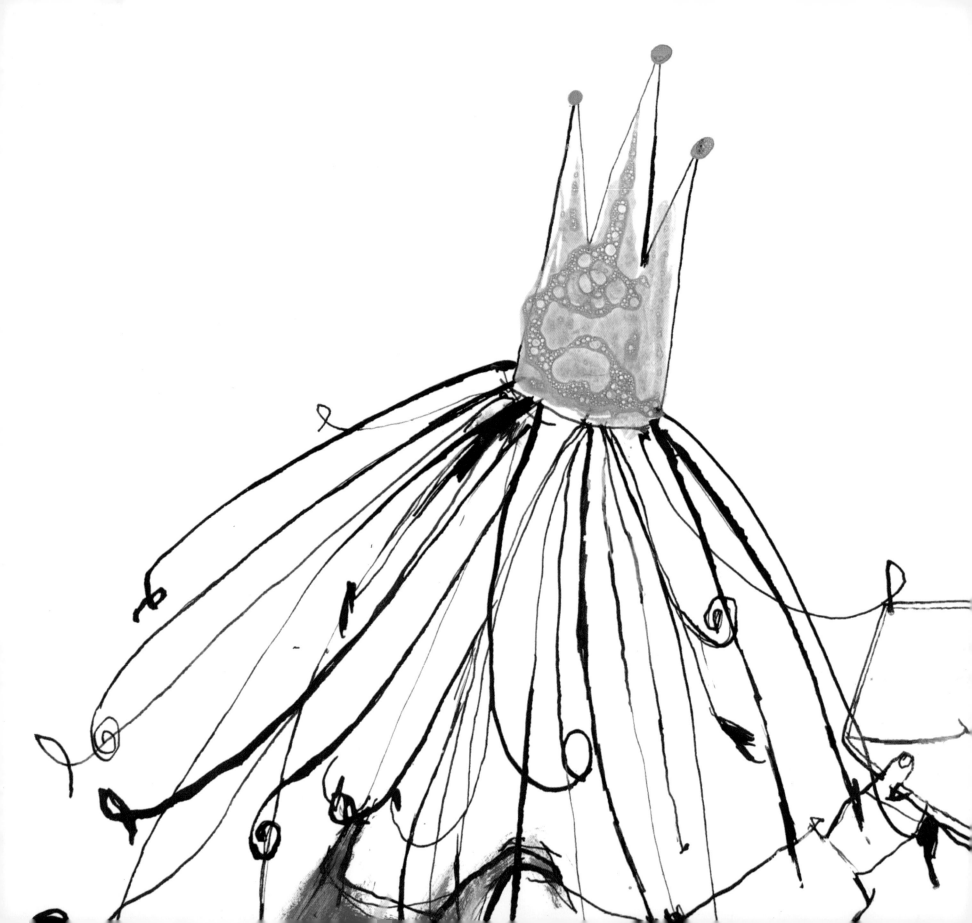

She chose one, Kvitebjørn, who had the friendliest eyes she had ever seen, and sent a letter back to him asking if they could meet some time.

They met in Princess Aasta's apple garden, and chased each other in between the trees.

Kvitebjørn picked apples for Princess Aasta from the top branches.

Princess Aasta and Kvitebjørn wanted to be together always.

The King

was worried about having

a **big,** dangerous

Ursus maritimus running about in his

garden.

But when he saw how much

fun the two of them had together,

he left them alone.

And when Kvitebjørn wanted to take Princess Aasta on a day trip to the North Pole, where he was from, the King couldn't say no. The King made them a packed lunch, and bade them a safe journey.

Princess Aasta climbed on to Kvitebjørn's back, and off they went, as far north as anyone can get. It was so beautiful up there, everything was covered in ice and snow. And Princess Aasta would never be cold, because Kvitebjørn's fur kept her warm.

Kvitebjørn introduced her to all his polar bear friends.

Afterwards, they went **ice-skating** and made an **enormous** snowman together.

And when northern lights appeared in the sky, it was time to go back to the King's castle.

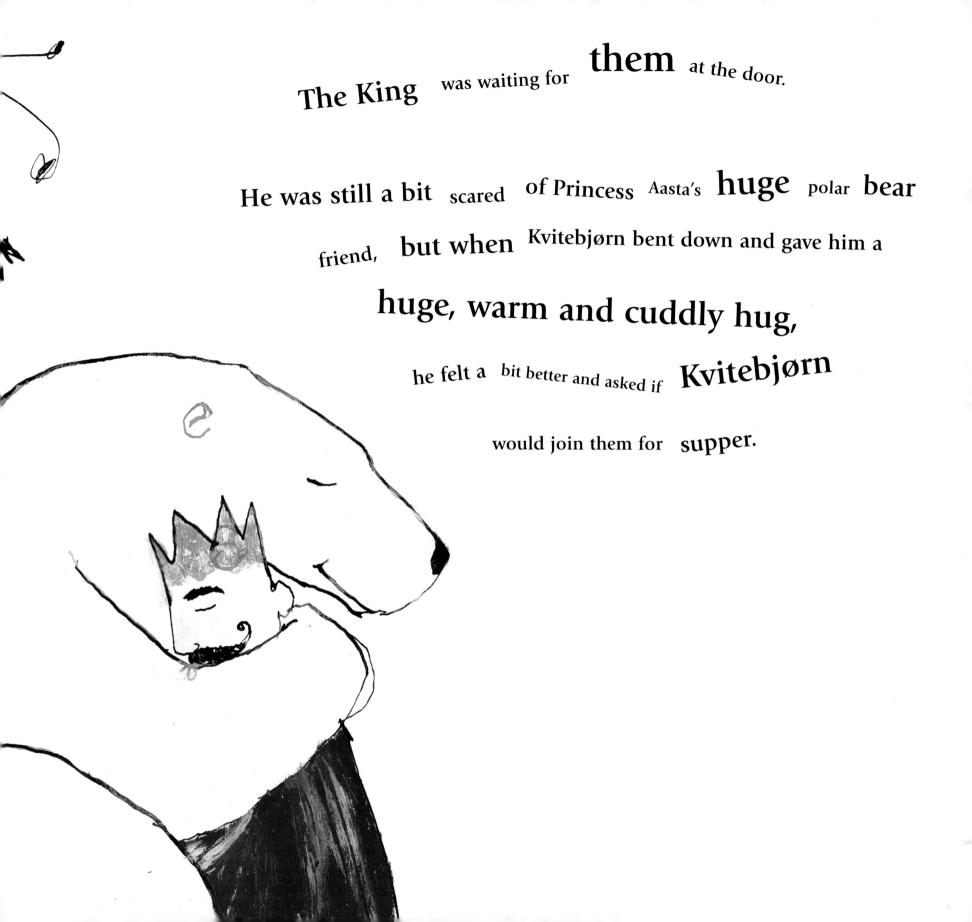

The King was waiting for them at the door.

He was still a bit scared of Princess Aasta's huge polar bear friend, but when Kvitebjørn bent down and gave him a huge, warm and cuddly hug, he felt a bit better and asked if Kvitebjørn would join them for supper.